# The Weakest
# Security Link Series

# The Weakest Security Link Series

## 1st Edition

*Luis F. Medina*
*IT Manager, Security Site Expert*
*CCNA, MCSE, MCP, Master CNE*

Writers Club Press
New York  Lincoln  Shanghai

The Weakest Security Link Series
1st Edition

Writers Club Press
an imprint of iUniverse, Inc.

For information address:
iUniverse
2021 Pine Lake Road, Suite 100
Lincoln, NE 68512
www.iuniverse.com

ISBN: 0-595-26494-8

Printed in the United States of America

I want to thank my Lord and Savior Jesus Christ for His faithfulness and for blessing my family with an opportunity to seek His kingdom first with our tithes and offerings, and to be future financial intercessors and bring hope to the hopeless.

I want to thank my family for their prayers and patience during this project and faith adventure. Yvette, (my wife), thanks for being a blessing in my life and for encouraging me to pursue my dreams. Matt and Gabe, (our sons), thanks for the opportunity to be parents to both of you. We are truly blessed!

I want to thank Pastor Robert Crosby, his staff, and the congregation at Mount Hope Christian Center for their commitment to God, people, prayer, and hope.

Finally, I want to thank www.thefishatlanta.com and www.klove.com for providing great songs over the Internet as I worked into the morning writing The Weakest Security Link series, 1st edition.

# Contents

Introduction

# The Weakest
# Security Link Series

**Introduction**

- In the absence of…
- Your company's network
- Join me on a journey
- About the Author
- Why this book?
- How this book helps You
- Predictions for 2003

In the absence of network security, exists an opportunity for intrusion. Your company's network security is only as strong as its weakest security link.

Join me on a journey to explore and identify the weak security links in your computer network(s). This book offers over 100 security tips to improve your network security today!

## About the Author

I have been supporting multi-platform (Unix, NT, NetWare, Windows 2000, and Mac OS) networks using TCP/IP protocol, Cisco infrastructure, and the Internet (combined) for over 15 years. This book contains network security tips that I use to protect critical production networks.

My security tips have also helped thousands of administrators secure their networks around the world.

## Why This Book?

Unlike other network security books written with in-depth coverage of things you don't need, this book takes a different spin on security: The focus of this book is to explore and identify the weak links in your network security. We will achieve this by addressing the basic and most overlooked security steps in your entire network. The goal of this series is to explore and identify weak security links in your entire network using your technology.

## How This Book Helps You

By focusing on your entire network security, this book is designed to save you time and effort in improving security. Anyone with a basic understanding of networking technology can benefit from this book. Some of the questions included in this book are thought provoking with the goal of getting you think seriously about security.

Many of you have written to me and provided very good feedback on my security series. Your feedback is what keeps making this series invaluable. To our new readers, expect plenty of more good (and advanced) security tips to improve your network in our upcoming second edition of the Weakest Security Link series (expected early 2004 or sooner, hopefully).

# Predictions for 2003

Recently, I was contacted to make a prediction for year 2003. Below is what I think is possible by hackers to achieve this year:

——- Original Message ——-
From: "Luis Medina" <netmgr@directvinternet.com>
To: "Fogarty, Susan" <SFogarty@techtarget.com
Sent: Thursday, December 19, 2002 9:38 AM
Subject: Re: what do you predict for 2003?

In 2003 and beyond, hackers will employ new methodologies and schemes to bring users indirectly to the hacker's attacks as opposed to bringing the attacks to network or remote users. Hackers will utilize new techniques and compromise websites (banks, universities, businesses, etc.) and transparently recruit users to involuntarily assist in a widespread attack against the compromised (above) websites.

The viable venue for a hacker's paradise will continue to be any application resident in memory on a server or host (with a port to spare) outside or behind a firewall. Hackers have written their thesis statement to the industry that no servers nor firewalls, nor desktops are out of their reach. They will continue to control the landscape that is the network that controls you.

The new security frontier will continue as an undeveloped field exposed to the dark forces of hackers and their clans. Network administrators will be left behind in the dust as they race on the road to recovery from another attack, this time caused by oblivious users visiting websites.

Hackers will continue to operate under the guise of normalcy to recruit hosts and gain an involuntarily start from users in developing their attacks. Another hacker will cross the bridge and surrender his identity to authorities and ask for redemption in an attempt to confound the wise.

I also predict that the least among all security books (hint, hint) will become one of the greatest security books over time—this too will confound the wise publishers.

Luis Medina

Online Support Incident

## The Weakest Security Link Series

| Online Support Incident |
|---|
| • Type of support<br>• Proof of purchase<br>• Limited time only<br>• Why include support? |

As an introductory offer to the Weakest Security Link series, We are offering one free security online support incident for a limited time only with the purchase of this book.

## Type of Support

The free security online support incident applies only for security related issues and for the technologies covered in this book. E-mail will be used as the default communication medium to address your security issue. The purpose of the free incident is to offer assistance in troubleshooting a security issue with your home or company network, and does not guarantee a solution; although, we will make every effort to solve the issue.

## Proof of Purchase

Proof of purchase of this book is required to use the one free security online support incident. To activate your support incident, visit our website and click on the e-mail icon. The URL is http://www.medinasystems.com.

## Limited Time Only

The free security online support incident is valid for only 30 days from the purchase of this book.

## Why Include Support?

The objective of this series is to explore and identify the security vulnerabilities in your network. As I write additional books in this series, you will find that this series will ultimately provide security tips for your entire network. Until then, we offer the online support incident to assist you with a security issue.

To extend support beyond the free security online support incident, you can contact us to purchase a block of additional support incidents.

# Chapter 1

# Combating Attacks

| Combating Attacks |
|---|
| • OSI Model |
| • Web-specific attacks |
| • Desktop-specific attacks |
| • Network-specific attacks |
| • 5-A Rule of Security |
| • Production Cisco router |
| • What if it's true? |

Combating web-specific and network attacks begins with an understanding of techniques used by hackers to penetrate your security, and the new technologies available to assist you in protecting your network using the OSI Model layered security approach.

Traditional firewalls and Intrusion Detection Systems (IDS) alone are no longer a viable solution for network security.

New tools are being developed to facilitate the attack process through new levels of automation and propagation. In addition, network-layer firewalls and Intrusion Detection Systems (IDS) do not detect web-specific or application layer attacks. They lack the proper filtering of specific web attacks and can only detect attacks based on known signatures using a single static database that requires updating on a regular basis. Application-layer firewalls exceed the level of security offered by traditional firewalls and Intrusion Detection Systems

1

(IDS). An application-layer firewall is tightly integrated into your web server to achieve greater security by embedding itself into the web server (e.g., IIS layer through ISAPI) and using numerous security filters. See chapter four (IIS 5 Web Server Security) for more information on IIS and ISAPI.

Hacking tools or programs not only automate the discovery process, but also detect security exploits at a faster speed than ever before. A hacking tool with automated capability and faster discovery process will enable a hacker to wreak havoc in your network, if the proper security technologies and measures are not in place, and if security is not properly maintained, monitored, and managed in a timely manner. If your company is proactive with network security, then security is an ongoing consideration in the design and planning phases of your network implementation and administration; your company has most likely:

- Designed and implemented layered security in a timely manner
- Adjusted and adapted to new technologies to address new attacks
- Maintained, monitored, and managed security measures.

If your company is reactive, security is an afterthought and a desperate measure to recover from an attack that can lead to unnecessary user and/or customer downtime, which can cost your company thousands or millions in damages; your company has most likely:

- Underestimated the importance of OSI model layered security approach.
- Neglected the need for new security technologies and proper measures.
- Overlooked ongoing security maintenance, monitoring, and management.

## OSI Model

The Open Systems Interconnect (OSI) model consists of 7 layers (Physical, Data Link, Network, Transport, Session, Presentation, and Application). The type of security associated with each layer is defined better by asking what potential attacks exist at each layer; below is a list of some of the attacks:

| | |
|---|---|
| Application attacks | Distributed DoS (DDoS) and spoofing |
| Presentation attacks | DDoS and spoofing |
| Session attacks | DDoS and spoofing |
| Transport attacks | DoS and hijacking |
| Network attacks | Spoofing of IP & poisoning of ARP |
| Data Link attacks | Overload of MAC table and port |
| Physical attacks | Sniffing and severing of backbone |

It is important that you understand that security is a moving target and requires ongoing attention and modifications to combat new attacks. (To help you keep in mind and recall security steps more easily, consider what I call Medina's 5-A Rule of Security later in this chapter)

## Web-specific Attacks (Application layer)

Directory Traversals

Directory traversals exist when a hacker invokes special characters to escape from the root folder using an improperly formed URL string in an attempt to access files stored in other folders resident on your web server. Ultimately, a hacker wants to peruse (e.g., using a relative directory path) through the file system structure of your web server. Web-based applications introduce another layer of inherent vulnerabilities due to poor coding and/or design flaws that can weaken the overall security of your web server. A hacker will often explore application exploits in an attempt to manipulate the designed or expected behavior of your web application, gain unauthorized access to your application, or access your data. This is why it is important for your company to implement and maintain a comprehensive layered security approach that incorporates a defense against all of the seven layers of the OSI model.

Buffer overflows/overruns

Buffer overflows exist when a hacker persistently sends data to your web server that causes copying of strings to exceed the maximum size of a buffer in an attempt to exploit a vulnerability and remotely run malicious code on your web server using the System account privilege. For example, a buffer overflow in an ISAPI extension (DLL program) will allow a hacker to execute code and take full control of your web server. No doubt, this intrusion will adversely affect—and temporarily change—the designed or expected behavior of your web server. Remember to inquire with your vendors regularly and obtain necessary patches developed to fix buffer overflow exploits. Don't limit your security maintenance updates to just the O/S and application levels, make sure that you address the seven layers of the OSI model when working with security.

| Security Tips |
| --- |
| • Install an application-layer firewall |
| • Move system command files off server |

Network-layer firewalls and IDS do not detect web-specific attacks. An application-layer firewall is tightly integrated into your web server to achieve greater security.

See chapter four for more information on application-layer firewalls.

Parsing attacks

A parsing attack exists when a hacker modifies a file request or string and changes the values by superimposing one or more operating system (O/S) commands via the request, then runs these commands, and gains unauthorized control of your web server to put or remove files remotely without authenticating. Parsing begins when hackers can execute the .bat (batch) or .cmd (command) file types on your web server. Combating web-specific and network attacks (see below) begins with your Cisco border router, the use of secured Access Control Lists (ACL), and Network-Based Application Recognition (NBAR) to filter traffic and limit common attacks to your servers.

Operating system and application security is a prerequisite if you want to effectively apply and maintain security using the OSI Model layer approach. Hence, the need for an application-layered firewall solution that works more closely with your web server application and compliments an existing network security. An application-layer firewall should address the above and other web-specific attacks. See chapter four (IIS 5 Web Server Security) for more information on application-layer firewalls.

## Desktop-specific Attacks

Recent attacks have circumvented firewall security via Internet browsers, e-mail applications, and file attachments. Users are no longer protected from hackers by a firewall or conventional security alone. The viable venue for a hacker's paradise is any application resident in memory on a host outside or behind a firewall. Hackers have sent a strong statement to the industry that no servers nor firewalls, nor desktops are out of their reach. They control the landscape that is the network that controls you. Regardless of a hacker's objective— whether to facilitate an attack from your computer to another site, or to obtain confidential information from your company, hackers are determined to go the distance and traverse your network seeking security vulnerabilities.

The new security frontier is an undeveloped field exposed to the forces of hackers. Attacks are designed to take advantage of misconfigured hosts running with outdated patches and missing critical security hot-fixes. Network administrators are left behind in the dust as they race on the road to recovery from another unnecessary attack. Malicious code (executable code) coupled with Trojan horses (destructive programs) operate under the guise of normalcy to recruit hosts and gain an involuntarily start from users. New attacks are difficult to detect as hackers utilize new methodologies to confound the wise all the while delivering a large-scale attack on the Internet.

To combat the existing desktop attacks, consider installing a desktop firewall on remote (VPN and dial-up) hosts. However, a desktop firewall is another application and, if misconfigured or not properly maintained, can become the weakest security link in your network. A desktop firewall should address the above and other desktop-specific attacks. See chapter 7 (Desktop Security) for more information on protecting your network and remote desktops.

# Network Attacks

IP Spoofing

IP spoofing occurs when a hacker alters the packet headers and falsifies the source IP address of a trusted host in your private network, and then infiltrates your network with his or her pseudo (bogus) host. Although IP spoofing is not a new technique, this method is still being used today.

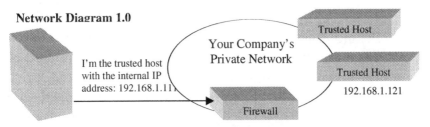

Outdated/improperly configured firewall

Anti spoofing begins with your border router and also with your Internet Service Provider (ISP). Check with your ISP to confirm (and don't assume) that they have implemented anti-spoofing on their routers (that provides the Internet uplink) to your perimeter (also known as border) router. When was the last time that you checked your router and firewall configurations to confirm that settings are in place to protect your network from IP spoofing?

**Network Diagram 1.1**

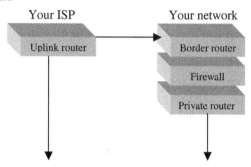

| Security Tips |
| --- |
| • Discard illegal packets<br>• Turn on anti-spoofing<br>• Test and apply hotfixes<br>• Provision your routers |

Discard all incoming packets on the external interface of the router and the firewall that are using the source IP address of a trusted host on your private network, to reduce the threat of inbound IP spoofing attacks.

Turn on anti-spoofing protection in your border routers and firewalls to strengthen your company's perimeter security. Ensure that your anti-spoofing parameters are properly configured and make sure that you guard against the potential of inbound spoofing attacks across all of your Internet (also known as Uplink) routers and your firewalls.

Test and apply the recent service packs and security hotfixes to patch any security holes. Be alert and understand that if you don't take care of your routers and firewalls, eventually a hacker will! (Check out my sample Cisco configuration file of a live production router at the end of this chapter with security tips to limit the effects of IP spoofing and denial of service (DoS) attacks.)

Did you know that new tools are being developed and Quality Assurance (QA) tested underground to assist hackers to launch an attack in your company's network(s)? Your failure to address these often-overlooked security areas, in a timely manner, will eventually allow a hacker to respond to the challenge with intrusion.

Denial of Service (DoS) Attacks

A DoS attack occurs when a hacker floods your network with repetitive packet requests (e.g. ICMP, UDP, etc.) to create unnecessary network congestion and deny network resources to affected users. The hacker's objective is to cause a service outage that will disrupt network communications within your infrastructure, cease server uptime availability, and prevent delivery of services to desktops. Improperly configured routers and the lack of security hotfixes allow hackers to exploit these areas and eventually launch one of several DoS attacks (e.g. sync-based, ping-based, distributed-based, etc.) against your network. In addition, different DoS types have different results, such as causing a buffer overflow in your router, running scripts in your computer's memory, or using your server's disk space as a central repository for sharing files on the Internet.

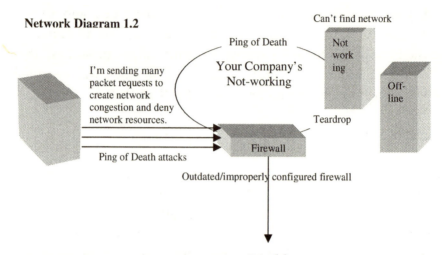

**Network Diagram 1.2**

| Security Tips |
| --- |
| • Disable extra services |
| • Configure ACL's! |
| • Review your config |
| • Monitor your logs |
| • Check protocol statistics |

Disable unnecessary services (e.g., echo) in your routers and firewalls to limit the damage of DoS attacks. Configure ACL's for both inbound and outbound traffic filtering across your perimeter defense layer. Avoid using default or one-size-fits-all values.

Review your router and firewall configuration and make the appropriate modifications to improve your network security. Know the services that your routers and firewalls are running and apply the relevant service packs and security hotfixes to patch known or new exploits. Make sure that you test new patches in a staging environment and avoid running in a live production network first.

Monitor your logs closely and carefully investigate any suspicious probes or activities occurring in your network. Check protocol statistics periodically and report any strange traffic patterns to your ISP immediately. Be alert and understand your normal network traffic patterns 24/7/365, which will become your baseline and assist you when you detect network congestion or a potential attack.

Worm Attacks

A worm attack occurs when a hacker infects your computer or network using a program with malicious code, for example, Nimda. This program replicates itself and propagates from infected networks to other networks on the Internet with the intent of collapsing part (or most) of the Internet. This type of attack spreads through email, html documents, and network shares.

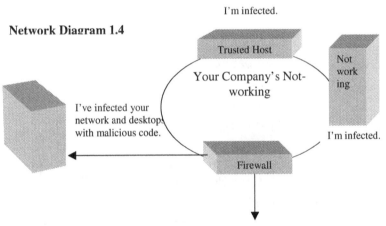

**Network Diagram 1.4**

Outdated/improperly configured firewall

| Security Tips |
| :---: |
| • Configure NBAR |
| • Specify packet criteria |
| • Filter by string |
| • Review sample config |
| • Apply security updates |

Configure Network-Based Application Recognition (NBAR) in your Cisco routers to limit WORM attacks. Specify packet criteria list and discard HTTP packets based on your patterns. Filter by MIME types, URL strings, and hostname strings. Apply security updates.

## Medina's 5-A Rule of Security

Medina's 5-A Rule of Security is Address, Adjust, Apply, Adapt, and Avoid:

1. Address new threats to your layered security.
2. Adjust security to combat new attacks.
3. Apply updates to maintain security.
4. Adapt new security technologies.
5. Avoid security compromise.

How do you know that a hacker hasn't already obtained unauthorized access to your company network or home computer? Let's start by examining the known techniques utilized by many hackers today, and the strategies to combat each security threat. To reiterate, not keeping up with security updates defeats the purpose of establishing security in the first place. Security updates are released to address specific vulnerabilities that usually allow some level of unauthorized access to a server due to poorly written code.

Most network administrators overlook the need to consistently apply security updates or hotfixes and therefore put the server or site at risk for potential attacks. Hackers probe for security vulnerabilities and then circumvent the site's security by gaining unauthorized access through open security leaks overlooked or software misconfiguration. For more information on production router and firewall secured configurations, see Appendix B with security tips on how to configure Network-Based Application Recognition (NBAR). If your Cisco *startup-config* file lacks the rules in the sample file listed below, then you have found your first weak security link. Remember to make a backup of your existing *running-config* file before making any changes to your routers and firewalls.

Let's examine the sample configuration file of my live production Cisco router. Only anti-spoofing, anti-DoS, and NBAR lines will be covered, therefore this is a partial file; it assumes that you understand how to install an ACL.

## Production Cisco Router Configuration

Although you can add separate deny rules, an implicit "deny ip any any" rule is added to the end when you use permit rules. The latter is better since you don't have to add a deny rule for every port you want to block.

For example, bind access-group 112 to external interface for inbound filtering:

```
interface <external interface>
ip address <external IP address> <subnet mask>
ip access-group 112 in
service-policy in anti-http
<interface speed>
```

This is an anti-spoofing and anti-DoS tip that prevents hackers from using PING to your network from a spoofed source IP address and creating unnecessary network congestion:

```
no ip directed-broadcast
```

This is an anti-HTTP tip that blocks HTTP packets by MIME types, URL strings, or hostname strings through NBAR and ACL. Repeat "match protocol" rule for additional strings:

```
class-map match-any <your criteria name> ! For example, anti-http
match protocol http url "<your executable>" ! For example,
*cmd.exe
policy-map <your policy criteria name>
class anti-http ! From class-map
ip dscp 1
```

This is another anti-HTTP tip that denies incoming HTTP packets with "cmd.exe" executables:

```
access-list 112 deny ip any any dscp 1 log
```

This is an anti-spoofing tip that denies incoming packets that use source IP addresses from your private network/subnet:

```
access-list 112 deny ip <your network> <inverted mask> any log
```

This is an anti-spoofing tip that denies incoming multicast packets:

```
access-list 112 deny ip 224.0.0.0 31.255.255.255 any log
```

This is an anti-spoofing tip that denies incoming localhost packets:

access-list 112 deny ip 127.0.0.0 0.255.255.255 any log

This is an anti-DoS tip that prevents attackers from sending ICMP echo requests. Make sure that you restrict PING to specific outside hosts to your internal servers:

access-list 112 permit icmp host <outside host> host <your server> echo log

This is an anti-DoS tip that prevents hackers from using your private network per RFC 1918. Deny incoming packets from reserved private networks.

access-list 112 deny ip 10.0.0.0 0.255.255.255 any log
access-list 112 deny ip 172.16.0.0 0.15.255.255 any log
access-list 112 deny ip 192.168.0.0 0.0.255.255 any log

This is a general security tip that denies hackers from initiating a connection from outside your network; only connections created from inside your network are permitted. Don't even think about installing an ACL if this line is not one of your rules. Inbound access is permitted back through the perimeter security only when the connection is initiated from inside your perimeter first.

access-list 112 permit tcp any <your network> <inverted mask> established log

This rule allows domain name resolution so network users can browse the Internet; If possible, limit this rule to your ISP's DNS servers:

access-list 112 permit udp any eq domain any log

Did you pass the test? Does your Cisco border/perimeter router config-uration already include the above rules? If yes, kudos! If not, you have some work to do to improve the security of your perimeter defense layer. Remember to test and stage your changes before applying in a production or live network. Always make a backup of scheduled and/or ad hoc modifications. Make sure that you do not support NetBIOS over TCP/IP (port 139) or SMB (port 445) in your border router or firewall; these ports are not secured and should be blocked from inbound or outbound access for security reasons. To allow these ports through would defeat the purpose of having a firewall in the first place.

Consider taking a minute to review the network diagram below, which depicts the Internet zone, Internet Service Provider (ISP) zone, your perimeter defense zone, and the demarcation line to your private net-work(s).

**Network diagram 1.5**

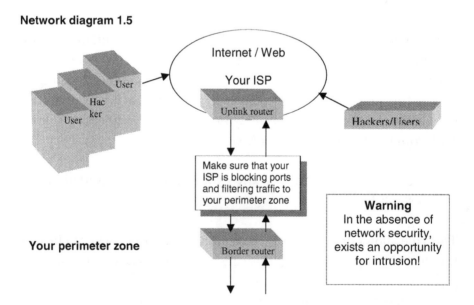

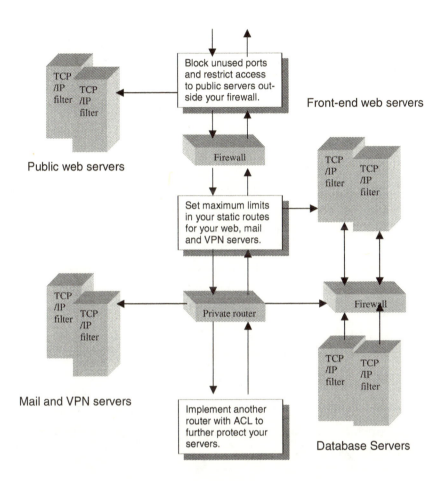

Having knowledge of all of the various public and private zones will help you to identify weak security links within your company's network infrastructure. Typically, you would not connect your border router with a crossed RJ45 cable to your firewall if you planned to set up redundancy links or public web servers outside your firewall. You would use a managed switch to allow additional connections for routers and/or public web servers.

The purpose of my book is to explore the various areas in your network and bring to the surface any security vulnerabilities that have been over-looked. The intention of this chapter is not to tell you how to set up a router or infrastructure, but to point out the often-overlooked security areas you should be aware of when configuring a secured router.

## What If It's True?

Have you ever wonder about the origin of the Internet and how it got started in the first place? The origin of the Internet can be found back in 1858 with the first deployment of the Atlantic cable across the ocean to handle real-time communications. Today, the Internet is a vital global communication medium used across many different cultures. But, is the time you spend online at work helping or hurting your business relationship with your company or customers?

In an Information Age, where knowledge is viewed by many as power, will the Internet or the information super-highway be a dead-end trip to the dreaded Tower of Babel? Has your real-time communication with your God turned into another destination along one of the cor-rupted path of the World Wide Web? Is the Internet a red herring in your relationship with God? Is your search engine finding the things of God or the things of this world?

What if it's true that the Internet is uniting scattered users over the face of whole earth in the 21st century using one common computer lan-guage (TCP/IP suite)? Although the Internet can be used for good, never in the history of the world has the invitation to sin been so widespread and easily accessible online. Your enemy is one mouse-click away—on standby 24/7/365 days—and lurks around the Internet seeking to steal your identity and destroy your testimony. Do you have a communica-tion link to God or is there a firewall blocking your path?

# Chapter 2

# Cisco Router & PIX Security

| Router Security |
| :---: |
| • Security is perennial<br>• Block unused ports<br>• Disable CDP<br>• Manage versions<br>• Router configuration<br>• PIX security |

You're the IT manager and have concerns about the security of your network. You've installed an Access Control List (ACL) on your border routers; you've installed a firewall and an Intrusion Detection System (IDS), an anti-virus system, and applied all of the required patches and security hotfixes to protect your network from hackers, right?

If you're confident that you have covered all of your bases, think again! In this chapter, we will focus on router and firewall security.

## Security is Perennial

Network security is a perennial task that requires ongoing modifications and appropriate adjustments to combat new forms of network attacks. In the absence of security, there is opportunity for intrusion. The focus of this book is to address the security weak links in your network, and the security risks overlooked by network users, administrators, and engineers.

## Block Unused Ports

Now that you have a better understanding of the different types of attacks, let's secure your company's first and second line of defense (that is, your Cisco border router and PIX firewall)—it makes sense to start here. Check with your hosting provider to see if they can add an access control list (ACL) on their router (which provides the Internet uplink) to your perimeter router. Have them block any port that your company does not require. The farther (hops) away from your network the filtering is done, the less traffic there will be on your network.

## Disable CDP

Avoid using default ports whenever possible and disable unnecessary protocols, whether it's at Layer 2 (e.g., CDP) or any other layer of the Open Systems Interconnect (OSI) model. I recommend that you read this chapter even if you are an administrator or engineer and understand TCP/IP ports, access control lists, etc. I am confident that you will find a security weak link in your network—after all, your network security is only as strong as your weakest security link.

How confident are you with the existing configuration of your Cisco router? If your *startup-config* file lacks the services or rules in the sample configuration file listed below then you have found your first security weak link.

# Manage IOS Versions

Although I don't consider an outdated IOS version (e.g. 12.5) to be a security issue—it's been my experience new releases are sometimes unreliable or include security holes—if your existing version has known security issues, then you should look into the next stable IOS version. In either case, you should keep a copy of your running-config file in another location to fall back on, if necessary.

| Security Tips |
| --- |
| • Deny outside VTY's |
| • Block outside telnet |
| • Use VPN access |
| • Restrict admin access |
| • Limit internal access |
| • Good password mgmt. |
| • Physical security |

Deny all VTY's. Disable outside access (even to restricted hosts) to your router's external and internal interfaces. Your router will still accept a session on port 23 on the inside interface, unless you block outside telnet to both interfaces. Use a VPN or dial-up connection to your network, and then access your router from inside.

Avoid the "too-many-hands-in-the-cookie-jar" syndrome. Restrict admin roles to one or two administrators and define the IP address of no more than two hosts that can access the router. These hosts should not run any public services or be exposed to the Internet. Use good password management to protect your router against unauthorized access by inside users. Restrict physical (console port) access to the router. A quick reboot and then the BREAK signal provides the inside culprit with control to your router.

Since you are not allowing external access to your router via Telnet, HTTP, or SNMP, it is less likely that a packet sniffer will obtain your passwords or network information. The more you protect against using unencrypted sessions over the Internet, the less likely it is for a potential intruder to hijack your connections and, ultimately, your router.

As you know, some protocols and services or applications are inherently insecure and pose a security risk to the company, your network, and your career. Ask yourself if you or your superiors are prepared to deal with the consequences associated with a security threat. To reiterate, in the absence of security, there is an opportunity for intrusion.

Let's examine the Cisco router sample configuration file. Only security related sections will be covered, therefore this is a partial file; it assumes you understand how to install an ACL.

## Router Configuration

Bind access-group 112 for inbound packet filtering. Make sure to only enable the services that are absolutely required; disable all others. Make it a point to understand the role of each service running in your Cisco routers. Below is a list of sample services:

This service uses basic algorithm to encrypt enable password:

```
service password-encryption
```

Avoid using these services (DEC): Discard, Echo, and Chargen:

```
no service tcp-small-servers
no service udp-small servers
```

Disable the finger and Cisco discovery protocol to prevent router from broadcasting (that is sending) information about itself to other devices:

```
no service finger
no cdp running
no cdp enable
```

Make sure that you disable http and SNMP access for remote configuration and monitoring. Also, encrypt your password, disable http to your router, and define your syslog server.

This next line uses MD5 password hashing for administrator account access:

```
enable secret 5 <password>
```

Avoid sending cleartext password or the equivalent, disable http server:

```
no ip http server
```

If you haven't set up a server, Kiwi Syslogd is pretty good:

```
logging <syslog server>
```

Don't even think about installing an access-list if this next line is not one of your rules. This next rule allows inbound access only when the connection is initiated from an inside host:

```
access-list 112 permit tcp any <your network> <inverted mask>
established log
```

This rule allows domain name resolution so users can browse the Internet. If possible, limit this rule to your ISP's DNS servers:

access-list 112 permit udp any eq domain any log

Restrict pings from specific outside hosts to your servers. The implicit deny rule in effect when you use an access list will deny other icmp types:

access-list 112 permit icmp host <outside host> host <your server> echo log

It's important to note that some services such as FTP use more than one TCP port. If you have to use FTP, change default ports of 21 and 20 (data), whenever possible.

The next rule permits any hosts on the Internet to connect to your SSL server:

access-list 112 permit tcp any host <your server> eq 443 log

The firewall adds an implicit deny rule after your permit rules; no need to add this line. When limiting inbound access, make sure you open up the appropriate ports for VPN:

access-list 112 deny ip any any

Did you pass the test? Does your Cisco perimeter/border router configuration already include the above rules? If yes, kudos! If not, you have some work to do to improve the security of your perimeter defense layer. Remember to test and stage your changes before applying in a production or live network. Always make a backup of scheduled or ad hoc modifications. Make sure that you do not support NetBIOS over TCP/IP (port 139) or SMB (port 445) in your border router or firewall; this port is not secured and should be blocked from inbound or outbound access for security reasons. To allow these ports through would defeat the purpose of having a border router or firewall in the first place.

| PIX Security |
| :---: |
| • Latest traffic volume<br>• 2nd level of defense<br>• Limit max connections<br>• Manage IOS versions<br>• Know your policy<br>• PIX configuration |

You've implemented a firewall with a good security policy to protect your production or corporate network, but do you know your security baseline? When was the last time you checked your firewall logs and updated your baseline to reflect the latest network traffic volume to your servers? Make sure you set embryonic limits in your static routes.

## Latest Traffic Volume

Why is it important to understand the latest traffic volume to your servers? Why allow unlimited connections in the firewall to your SMTP server, if your syslog server has never logged more than 100 simultaneous connections to the mail server?

Why allow more connections in the firewall to your Outlook Web Access (OWA) server than configured OWA users? These are just two servers (out of many) that can benefit from an embryonic limit. Your PIX firewall policy should reflect the minimum connection requirements (with some room for growth) of your servers, where the value of "max_conns" and "em_limit' is NOT set to unlimited.

# 2nd Level of Defense

The firewall is your company's second level of defense against hackers on the Internet. Yet, most "out-of-the-box" firewall configurations support unlimited connections to your servers via static routes, and, for example, in the case of PIX firewall version 5.34, unlimited incomplete (embryonic) connections are supported by default. In other words, your servers are susceptible to a flood attack, unless you set an appropriate embryonic limit in your static entry for each server.

## Limit Max Connections

Set limits on your static routes and avoid using the unlimited default value. There is no "one-size-fits-all" setting when it comes to the maximum connections and/or embryonic limits in the firewall for your servers—perhaps this explains why Cisco PIX defaults to unlimited for both settings. Administrators should extrapolate the information necessary to arrive at a conclusion from the firewall and server logs. If you haven't checked your firewall logs recently, now would be a good time to do so and begin to establish a security baseline and improve your firewall security policy.

If your PIX firewall policy accepts unlimited connections or has no embryonic limits defined for your servers, then you have found your first security weak link. Below is a sample configuration file to improve the security of your firewall. Remember to make a backup of your firewall and test your security rules.

# Know Your Policy (PIX Firewall Configuration)

This is a partial sample file of a live production firewall; it assumes you understand how to install an access list. Let's examine the sample firewall configuration and policy:

Sample PIX 5.34 Firewall config:

See static entries below for maximum and embryonic limits
nameif ethernet0 outside security0
nameif ethernet1 inside security100
enable password <PWD>encrypted
passwd <PWD> encrypted
hostname <HOSTNAME>
fixup protocol ftp 21
fixup protocol http 80
fixup protocol h323 1720
fixup protocol rsh 514
fixup protocol smtp 25
fixup protocol sqlnet 1521
fixup protocol sip 5060
no fixup protocol rtsp 554
names

Note: Access list for servers defined in static list below:

access-list outside_in permit tcp any host <YOUR MAIL SERVER> eq smtp
access-list outside_in permit tcp any host <YOUR OWA SERVER> eq 443
access-list outside_in permit tcp any host <YOUR IIS SERVER> eq 80

```
no pager
logging on
logging timestamp
no logging standby
no logging console
no logging monitor
no logging buffered
logging trap informational
no logging history
logging facility 22
logging queue 512
logging host inside <SYSLOG>
interface ethernet0 100full
interface ethernet1 100full
mtu outside 1500
mtu inside 1500
ip address outside <INTERFACE> <MASK>
ip address inside <INTERFACE> <MASK>
ip verify reverse-path interface outside
ip audit info action alarm
ip audit attack action alarm
no failover
failover timeout 0:00:00
failover poll 15
failover ip address outside 0.0.0.0
failover ip address inside 0.0.0.0
arp timeout 14400
global (outside) 1 interface
nat (inside) 1 0.0.0.0 0.0.0.0 0 0
```

Note: Maximum connection is set to 100 and embryonic to 25 for SMTP & OWA servers:

static (inside,outside) <Valid IP> <YOUR MAIL SERVER> netmask
255.255.255.255 100 25
static (inside,outside) <Valid IP> <YOUR OWA SERVER> netmask
255.255.255.255 100 25
static (inside,outside) <Valid IP> <YOUR IIS SERVER> netmask
255.255.255.255 1000 100

access-group outside_in in interface outside
route outside 0.0.0.0 0.0.0.0 <default gateway> 1
timeout xlate 3:00:00
timeout conn 1:00:00 half-closed 0:10:00 udp 0:02:00 rpc 0:10:00 h323
0:05:00 si
p 0:30:00 sip_media 0:02:00
timeout uauth 0:05:00 absolute
aaa-server TACACS+ protocol tacacs+
aaa-server RADIUS protocol radius
no snmp-server location
no snmp-server contact
snmp-server community public
no snmp-server enable traps
floodguard enable
no sysopt route dnat
isakmp identity hostname
terminal width 80

Did you pass the test? Do your Cisco PIX firewall configuration
includes the above rules? If yes, kudos! If not, you have some work to do
to improve the security of your 2nd layer of defense. Remember to test
and stage your changes before applying in a production or live network.
Always make a backup of scheduled or ad hoc modifications.

The purpose of my book is to explore the various areas in your network and bring to the surface any security vulnerabilities that have been overlooked. The intention of this chapter is not to tell you how to set up a firewall, but to point out the areas you should be aware of when configuring a Cisco PIX firewall.

## What If It's True?

The tragedy of 9/11 is proof enough that terrorists do not appreciate the freedom that we enjoy as Americans. As long as we remain an open society, terrorists will target us. America is prepared to defend freedom at any cost.

While we cannot change the past, we can learn from it and embrace the present and the future. We must invest in advanced security at all of our airports, especially, international airports. New technology should be implemented to easily detect radioactive, anthrax, and sophisticated plastic weapons.

We must demand better communication between the Central Intelligence Agency and the Federal Bureau of Investigation to interrupt terrorist plans of attack against Americans on U.S. soil, and develop better border patrol across the U.S to ensure terrorists don't enter from other countries.

What if it's true that a global database will help track and trace various terrorist patterns of activities in the U.S. and on the Internet from groups in other countries?

# Chapter 3

# — Windows 2000 Server Security

| Windows 2000 Security |
| --- |
| • Windows 2000 services |
| • Network connections |
| • TCP/IP filtering |
| • Local security policy |
| • IP Security (IPSec) |
| • NLB as firewall |
| • EFS using Cipher |
| • Windows components |
| • Automatic Updates |
| • Registered extensions |
| • Windows font viewer |
| • Code page conversion |
| • System |
| • Active Directory |
| • Com Internet services |
| • Computer Mgmt. |
| • DNS Server |
| • QoS |
| • Dr. Watson |
| • Filer Signature (Sigverif) |
| • Driver Mgr. (Verifier) |

It's not inconceivable for a Windows 2000 Server to have up to 80 services or more either running (set to automatic type) or ready to run (set to manual type) upon startup. Your server configuration will require that some services are started, but it is unlikely that your server will require that all of the 80 services be running. Therefore, it is important for security reasons that all of the other unnecessary services (i.e., Remote Registry, RunAs, Server, etc.) be stopped and disabled.

The more services that are running, the greater the potential for a security breach against the server. With that said, let's examine the Windows 2000 services. It's important to test the response of the server after stopping each service since you will lose some functionality. Stop the following services and change the service type to manual, upon successful server startup, change the service type to disable:

## Windows 2000 Services

Alerter

Application Management

Automatic Updates

Background Intelligence

Clipbook

Computer Browser

DHCP Client

Distributed File System

Distributed Link Tracking System

Distributed Link Tracking Server

Distributed Transaction Coordinator

DNS Client

Fax Service

File Replication Service

IIS Admin Service

Indexing Service

Internet Connection Sharing

Intersite Messaging

Logical Disk Manager

Messenger

Microsoft Search

Net Logon

NetMeeting Desktop Sharing

Network Connections

Network News Transport Protocol

Plug and Play

Print Spooler

Print Spooler

Remote Procedure Call (RPC)

Remote Procedure Locator

Remote Registry

Removal Storage

Server

SMTP

Task Scheduler

TCP/IP NetBIOS Helper

Telephony

Telnet

Terminal Services

Windows Management

Windows Management Driver

Windows Media Monitor Service

Windows Media Program Service

Windows Media Station Service

Windows Media Unicast Service

Windows Time

Workstation

WWW Publishing Service

# Network and Dial-up Connections

Prevent access on TCP port 139 and 445 to your server. Disable "Client for Microsoft Networks" and "File and Printer Sharing for Microsoft Networks" by going to the General tab of the Local Area Connection Properties and making sure both check boxes are cleared.

# TCP/IP Filtering

To enable TCP/IP filtering, go to the General tab of TCP/IP Properties and click on the Advanced button, then Options tab, select TCP/IP filtering, click on the Properties button, and then click on "Enable TCP/IP Filtering (All adapters)" check box. Next, select "Permit only" for TCP Ports, UDP Ports, and IP Protocols. Finally, enter the ports (e.g., 443) and protocol version (e.g., ipv6) that your server will support.

# Local Security Policy

In Administrative Tools, launch the Local Security Policy program to define your Account Policies (password, lockout, kerberos), Local Policies (audit, user rights, security), and IP Security Policies. Let's begin by creating an IPSec policy with filter and filter action:

IPSec Policy: Install a policy to restrict access to your server.

To launch the policy wizard, right-click on IP Security Policies on Local Machine and select "Create IP Security Policy". After you have entered a name for your policy, deselect "Activate the default response rule". Add a new security rule (using security rule wizard), do not specify a tunnel, select LAN for network type, use Windows 2000 Kerberos V5 protocol, and then click on the Add button to create a new filter list. Next, choose

"Any IP Address" for traffic source, "My IP Address" for traffic destination, select the protocol type (e.g., ICMP), click on the Next button and check the Edit properties check box. Make sure that "Mirrored" is selected and click on the OK button to return to the IP Filter List. Click on Close button to return to the Security Rule Wizard. (You will notice that your filter is listed with ALL ICMP traffic and All IP Traffic.) Select your IP filter, click on the Next > button, in Filter Actions, click on the Add button to define (and name) your filter action, select Block, then click on the Next > button and make sure Edit properties is checked.

Let's add another port (TCP 80) to block in your newly created IPSec policy. Right-click on IP Security Policies on Local Machine and select "Manage IP filter lists and filter actions", go to Manage IP filter tab, click on the Edit button and then Add button to start the IP Filter Wizard. Specify the traffic source (any IP), destination (my IP), TCP for protocol, and enter the range of 80 (from this port) to 80 (to this port). You are now blocking ICMP and HTTP in your IPSec policy. Consider adding a tunnel for secure communications between your internal servers.

Congratulations, you have successfully created your first IP filter with filter action. Repeat the above steps to add additional filters, ports, and actions.

Account Policies/Password Policy

- Do not enforce password history.
- Set maximum password age to 30 days.
- Set minimum password age to 0 days.
- Set minimum password length to 12 characters.
- Require password meet complexity requirements.
- Store password using reversible encryption.

Account Policies/Account Lockout Policy

- Set account lockout duration to 60 minutes.
- Set account lockout threshold to 3 attempts.
- Reset account lockout counter after 60 minutes.

Account Policies/Kerberos Policy

- Enforce user logon restrictions.
- Set maximum lifetime for service ticket to 480 minutes.
- Set maximum lifetime for user ticket to 8 hours.
- Set maximum lifetime for user ticket renewal to 10 days.
- Set maximum tolerance for computer clock synchronization to 3 minutes.

Local Policies/Audit Policy

- Audit account logon events for failed attempts.
- Audit account management for successful and failed attempts.
- Audit directory services access for successful and failed attempts.
- Audit logon events for failed attempts.
- Audit object access for failed attempts.
- Audit policy change for successful and failed attempts.
- Audit privilege use for successful and failed attempts.
- Audit process tracking for failed attempts.

Audit system events for failed attempts.

In the next section of local policy settings, you will notice that access is assigned to native user groups (i.e., Administrators, Power Users, Everyone) by default. Consider adding unique group names or individual users and removing the existing privileges assigned to default groups; avoid using the group Everyone and default user accounts. I've included below the critical sections to address when planning your server security. Replace or remove Administrators, Backup Operators, Power Users, Users, Everyone from the following assignments:

Local Policies/User Rights Assignment

- Access this computer from the network.
- Back up files and directories.
- Bypass traverse checking.
- Change the system time.
- Create a page file.
- Debug programs.
- Enable accounts trusted for delegation.
- Force shutdown from a remote system.
- Increase quotas.
- Increase scheduling priority.
- Load and unload device drivers.
- Log on as a batch job.
- Log on locally.
- Manage auditing and security log.
- Modify firmware environment values.
- Profile single process.
- Profile system performance.
- Remove computer from docking station.
- Restore files and directories.
- Shut down the system.
- Take ownership of files or other objects.

Local Policies/Security Options

- Set additional restrictions for anonymous connections not to allow enumeration of SAM accounts and shares.
- Disable allow server operators to schedule tasks.
- Disable shut down without having to log on.
- Set amount of idle time required before disconnecting session to 7 minutes.
- Enable audit of global system objects.
- Enable audit use of backup and restore privilege.
- Enable automatic log off users when logon time expires (local).
- Clear virtual memory pagefile when system shuts down.
- Enable not to display last user name in logon screen.
- Set LAN manager authentication level to send NTLMv2 response only\refuse LM & NTLM.
- Add legal message for text for users attempting to log on.
- Add message title for users attempting to log on.
- Do not cache previous logons.
- Enable prevent system maintenance of computer account password.
- Enable prevent users from installing printer drivers.
- Set prompt user to change password before expiration to 7 days.
- Disable recovery console.
- Rename administrator account.
- Rename guest account.
- Enable restrict CD-ROM access to locally logged-on users only.
- Enable restrict floppy access to locally logged-on user only.
- Disable send unencrypted password to connect to third-party SMB servers.
- Enable shut down system immediately if unable to log security audits.

- Enable strengthen default permissions of global system objects.
- Do not allow installation of unsigned driver.
- Do not allow installation of unsigned non-driver.

## Local Group Policy (Administrative Templates)

Launch Group Policy (gpedit in system32) to customize the computer and user configuration. Confirm that "Computer configuration settings" and "User configuration settings" are not disabled, go to properties of Local Computer Policy and deselecting each check box. In Administrative Templates, disable NetMeeting/remote desktop sharing, then go to Internet Explorer and configure the following: (You should also configure these settings on Windows 2000 hosts.)

Internet Explorer

- Enable Security Zones (use only machine settings) to maintain consistency of security settings with other users on this machine.
- Enable Security Zones (do not allow users to change policies) to prevent users from changing security settings via slider.
- Enable Security Zones (do not allow users to add/delete sites) to prevent users from adding web sites to security zone.
- Enable Proxy setting per-machine to establish a uniform proxy setting and restrict users from configuring a user-specific proxy setting.
- Enable IE browser restriction of automatically installing components to prevent IE from downloading components from web sites.
- Enable restriction of periodic IE browser updates checks.

Task Scheduler

- Enable Hide Property Pages to prohibit users from modifying task properties.
- Enable Prevent Task Run or End to restrict users from manually running tasks.
- Enable restriction of Drag-and-Drop to prevent users from adding tasks.
- Enable restriction of New Task Creation to prohibit users from creating new tasks.

Windows Installer

- Enable restriction of the use of Windows Installer.

System/Logon

- Enable deletion of cached copies of roaming profiles.

## Local Group Policy (User Configuration)

Windows Settings

- Enable trusted publisher lockdown in Internet Explorer Maintenance.
- Set Remote Installation Services Choice Options to Deny for setups and tools.

Administrative Templates

- Enable Maximum bandwidth for Audio & Video in NetMeeting (if running).
- Enable restriction of security tab in IE browser.
- Enable "No Computers Near Me" in My Network Places.
- Enable "No Entire Network" in My Network Places.
- Enable "Restrict the user from entering author mode".
- Enable "Remove access to use all Windows Update features".
- Enable "Remove the Shut Down command".
- Enable "Disable the command prompt".
- Enable "Disable registry editing tools.

## IP Security (IPSec)

See Local Security Policies for instructions on how to create an IPSec policy, IP filter, and filter action. Use IP Security Monitor (ipsecmon in system32) to monitor IPSec statistics.

To enable IPSec, go to the General tab of TCP/IP Properties and click on Advanced button, Options tab, select IP Security, click on Properties button, and then click on "Use this IP security policy" box. Next, choose the IPSec policy you defined (above).

## Network Load Balancing (NLB) as a firewall

To secure your cluster configuration, go to Network and Dial-up Connections, right-click on Local Area Connection, and check the Network Load Balancing box. Next, click on Properties and enter the following information in the Cluster Parameters tab:

- Primary IP address.
- Subnet mask.
- Internet name.
- Enable multicast support (add static ARP in border router).

Disable remote control (i.e., remote use of wlbs command to stop, start, query, etc). In the Host Parameter tab, set priority ID to 1 on first server, ID to 2 on second server, and so on. Each server must have a unique IP address that you can use to access via secured remote control software.

| Security Tips |
|---|
| • Set NLB filtering mode to Multiple<br>• Set affinity to Single<br>• Disable filtering to use NLB as firewall |

In Port Rules tab, remove the default port range of 0 to 65535 and replace with specific ports. Enter each port and change the protocols (TCP, UDP, Both) state accordingly. Set filtering mode to multiple hosts with affinity set to single to load balance IP packets on the specific port(s) you entered above.

To use NLB as a mini firewall, remove all of the ports defined, enter the ports you want to block and set filtering mode to disabled.

## Encrypting File System (EFS) using Cipher

Use command-line program Cipher to encrypt your folders and files. Type "cipher" alone without qualifiers to display a list of folders and files encrypted (E) or unencrypted (U). Type "cipher /?" to get a list of parameters and command syntax to use; for example, /e = encrypt, /d =

decrypt, /s=includes subdirectories, and /k = create new file encryption key: Type cipher /e /s: "<directory or file name>.

| Security Tips |
|---|
| • Use Cipher to encrypt<br>• Avoid using drag-and-drop<br>  for files |

For example, "cipher /e /s: temp" sets the directory temp to encrypt new files created in this directory; however, files copied to the temp (or other encrypted) folders using drag-and-drop will not be encrypted, by default. Run the cipher command again.

## Windows Components

Remove unnecessary components (e.g., script debugger, accessories and utilities, etc.) from Add/Remove Programs.

## Automatic Updates

Avoid running the Windows Update Service to automatically update your server since this process can be hacked. If you decide to use this service, then set it to notify you before downloading and installing any update! Visit Security & Privacy section at www.microsoft.com/security and download the following tools to assist you with security updates:

- Baseline Security Analyzer: Scans your server for common security misconfiguration.
- HFNetChk: Command line tool that identifies the current patch level of your server and missing patches.
- IIS Lockdown: Disables unnecessary IIS features.

- URLScan: Works in conjunction with IIS Lockdown to restrict HTTP requests.

In addition to maintaining your operating system updated with the latest service pack and security hotfix, native and third-part applications and drivers need to be patched to address security holes.

## Registered Extensions

Delete registered file types (e.g., EML, HTT, HTW, HTX, JOB, JS, and XSL) in Folder Options that you don't plan to support. Consider removing all of the extensions and manually adding only the file types that you plan to use.

## Windows Font Viewer

Delete unnecessary fonts or encrypt the parent Fonts folder to secure data by clicking on the advanced tab of the properties of any font name. You will receive a warning box to encrypt the file and the parent folder. Click on the OK button. If you receive an error applying attributes, go to Fonts folder in the system root folder and assign "modify rights" to your account, then clear the read-only check box. Select apply changes to this folder.

## Code Page Conversion Tables

Uncheck unused code pages (currently about 114) box enabled by default in General tab of Regional Options. Click on Advanced button, select language and clear check; you will be able to remove all except for 30 (or so) code pages.

## System

Block any attempt to install unsigned drivers on your server in the Hardware tab. If necessary, manually unblock, install unsigned file, and then block again. In the Advanced tab, disable the following actions and change the default path for dump file:

- Display list of operating systems for any seconds.
- Send an administrative alert.
- Automatically reboot.
- Overwrite any existing file.

## Active Directory

Users and Computers

If you have upgraded your servers to Windows 2000 and are no longer running Windows NT or have any dependencies to NT, then consider changing the domain mode from mixed mode (pre-Windows 2000 support) to native mode on your domain controller. Right-click on the fully qualified domain, select Properties, and click on Change Mode button in the General tab. (You can also change mode in domains and trusts). In the Managed By tab, add/change the account to manage the domain.

Although you can't rename built-in groups or add to other groups, you can control which users are members. Remove unnecessary members from the following groups:

- Account Operators
- Administrators

- Backup Operators
- Guests
- Pre-Windows 2000
- Print Operators
- Replicator
- Server Operators
- Users

Avoid using "Trust computer for delegation" on a production Windows 2000 server that doesn't require a service from another server. Verify that the proper primary group (in Member Of tab) is set for your domain controller. In Users container, rename the Administrator account and disable unused and default accounts. Consider creating a restricted user account, naming it Administrator, and auditing for any failed login attempts to tip you off when a hacker appears on the scene. Below are some of the user and global group accounts that you definitely want to rename and minimize members to:

- Administrator
- Cert Publishers
- DNSAdmins
- Domain Admins
- Enterprise Admins
- Group Policy Creator Owners
- IUSR_<computer name>
- IWAM_<computer name>
- Schema Admins

Sites and Services

Check the permission assignments in the Security tab of the Sites container (and sub containers) and remove users and inheritable permissions to reflect your admin environment. Again, consider removing known or default groups and replacing accounts with unique groups or users instead. Modify the replication schedule for both NTDS and default IP Site Link connections. Create a subnet address for your site.

## COM Internet Services

Did you know that if a hacker executes the "dtcsetup" stand-alone program in the system32 folder it will stop your MS DTC service indefinitely and begin the copy process of MS DTC files? Move these types of programs off your servers.

To enable COM Internet Services, go to the Default Properties tab and click on check box to run "on this computer". At a minimum, change the default Authentication Level to Packet security and Impersonation Level to Impersonate. Enable "Provide additional security for reference tracking. In MSDTC tab, change the location and file name of the log file DTCLog.

| Security Tips |
| --- |
| • Use port range for DCOM<br>• Use Deny Default Access Permission |

Enter a TCP/IP port range for DCOM Intranet in the Default Protocols tab of My Computer in Component Services. Next, remove the other unused protocols. Then, go to Default Security tab, and edit "access permissions".

You may want to add the Administrators group and set type of access to "Deny DefaultAccessPermission", to prevent administrators from accessing your application. You can also use this permission in conjunction with "Allow DefaultAccessPermission" for other users. Consider removing Administrators from Default Launch Permissions also.

Set and test the following security changes for COM+ Applications. Make sure that you understand your application and external dependencies (to other applications) before making these modifications. You many need to tune the process settings (e.g., leave process running when idle or shut down the process) to find a secure and functional configuration that works in your environment. Included are some IIS components to assist you web server application.

Set COM+ QC DLQL to enforce access checks, to perform access checks at the process and component level, and to use packet for authentication level and impersonate for impersonation level. Specify a unique account and password in the Identity tab. Activate components in a dedicated server process. Set server process shutdown (in Advanced tab) when idle to 1 minute. Disable deletion and changes.

- Set IIS In-Process Applications to enforce access checks, to perform access checks at the process and component level, and enable authentication. Specify a unique account and password in the Identity tab. Activate components in a dedicated server process. Set server process shutdown when idle to 1 minute. Disable deletion and changes.

- Set IIS Out-Of-Process Pooled Applications to enforce access checks, to perform access checks at the process and component level, and to use packet for authentication level and impersonate for impersonation level. Specify a unique account and password in the Identity tab. Activate components in a dedicated server process. Set server process shutdown when idle to 1 minute. Disable deletion and changes.

- Set IIS Utilities to enforce access checks, to perform access checks at the process and component level, and to use packet for authentication level and impersonate for impersonation level. Activate components in a dedicated server process. Set server process shutdown when idle to 1 minute. Disable deletion and changes.

- Set—{Default Web Site//Root} to enforce access checks, to perform access checks at the process and component level, and to use packet for authentication level and impersonate for impersonation level. Specify a unique account and password in the Identity tab. Activate components in a dedicated server process. Set server process shutdown when idle to 1 minute. Disable deletion and changes.

- Set System Application to enforce access checks and use packet privacy for authentication level. Set server process shutdown when idle to 1 minute. Delete and customize the users assigned to roles.

- Set Workflow Event Sink to enforce access checks, to perform access checks at the process and component level, and to use packet for authentication level and impersonate for impersonation level. Activate components in a dedicated server process. Set server process shutdown when idle to 1 minute. Disable deletion and changes. Delete and customize the users assigned to roles.

Track transaction statistics in Distributed Transaction Coordinator.

# Computer Management (compmgmt)

Event Viewer

Once you have properly and securely configured your Windows 2000 Server, clear all of the event viewer logs, such as Application, Directory Service, DNS Server, File Replication Server, Security, and System. Next, set maximum log size to 7 MB and manually save your logs daily.

Performance Logs and Alerts

At a minimum, set Alerts for TCP and IP counters, right-click on Alerts and create a new alert setting. Track the following counters for TCP/IP and set alert for Over your custom limit (e.g., TCP connection failure to over 100). Set schedule to start and stop scan after-hours and write to application log.

- TCP Connection Failures
- TCP Connections Passive
- TCP Connections Reset
- IP Datagrams Outbound No Route
- IP Datagrams Received Address Errors
- IP Datagrams Received Header Errors
- IP Fragmentation Failures

Shared Folders

Stop sharing Address, ADMIN$, C$, IPC$, NETLOGON, and Resources$ and remove the group Everyone from your server's root drive. Whenever possible, replace the group Everyone with the group Authenticated Users. In addition, move programs (e.g., adminpak, dtc-setup, ddeshare, etc.) from the system32 folder and store on a CD-ROM onsite for administrative purpose. Delete DDE Shares and Trusted Shares using the DDE Share Manager.

Services and Applications

Consider making security changes to providers in your Telephony service. Right-click on Telephony service and select "Manage Providers" and remove unused providers. Next, right-click on Telephony service, select Properties to set a restricted user account. If you must use WMI services, in WMI Control, change the account to a unique account and the default log path and file name. Remove the group Everyone from the Root folder (in Security tab) and change the default folder for scripting (in Advanced tab) to another location. Secure Indexing Service by preventing index of files with unknown extension. Avoid adding network shares automatically. Select "Inherit above settings from Service" for System and Web properties

## DNS Server

If your Windows 2000 Server is running as dedicated DNS server, then consider making and testing the following security changes. Right-click DNS server to access its properties. In the Interfaces tab, select to listen on the server's IP address. Limit forwarders to your ISP's primary and cache DNS servers. Select "Fail on load if bad zone data" and to "Secure cache against pollution". If not using AD, set to load zone data from Registry on startup. Enable "automatic scavenging of stale records" to 5 day period. Remove unnecessary inheritable permissions to groups (e.g., Administrators and Domain Admins) and replace with individual user accounts or unique group names.

. (dot) and .com Properties

Allow only secure updates for dynamic updates, set the aging period (refresh interval) to 5 days, and enable scavenging of stale resource records. Avoid using WINS forward lookup. Do not allow zone transfers and replace default user groups with individual user accounts or unique groups. Avoid default accounts inheriting permissions.

## Quality of Service (QoS) Control (acssnap)

Using the QoS Admission Control, create a new policy or reservation for un-authenticated (anonymous) users connecting to IIS web server. For front-end servers communicating to back-end SQL servers set identity to User and select a restricted user account. Set the direction of flow to send and receive; depending on your uplink or backbone bandwidth, set and test the data rate (Kbits/sec), the peak data rate (Kbits/sec), and duration (minutes) for flow and aggregate limits, according to your company's requirements. Delete the default reservations that come with QoS.

## Dr. Watson (drwtsn32)

I don't recommend that you use Dr. Watson except when troubleshooting an intermittent application issue since sensitive information (such as user name or account logged in) can be dumped in the crash dump file. If you have to use Dr. Watson, change the default log file path and then move the crash file "user.dmp" that Dr. Watson for Windows 2000 uses from "C:\Documents and Settings\All Users.<server name>\ Documents\DrWatson" to a different folder location.

## File Signature Verification (sigverif)

Scan your server for changes made to digitally signed file daily. Select "Notify me if any system files are not signed" in the Search tab of the Advanced button. You will notice in the Logging tab, the default log file name "SIGVERIF.TXT"; change this file name to another name.

## Driver Verification Manager (verifier)

Verify system drivers in Settings tab using verification type (special pool, pool tracking, I/O, etc.). Also, monitor global counter statistics.

# Chapter 4

# IIS Web Server & Media Stream Security

**Web Server Security**

- Application-layer firewall
- Understanding ISAPI
- Administration web site
- IIS is not an FTP service
- Extension Mappings
- The Problem
- The Solution
- Media stream security

Is your web server security pukka? That is, is it authentic or a target for unauthorized access? Are you clustering servers but cluttering security, or are your web servers speaking in unity? If your border router or firewall could whisper a packet, would your web servers listen or block it? If so, are you in danger of a web server that welcomes an intruder? See chapter three (Windows 2000 Security) to implement operating system security before proceeding with IIS security.

Web servers are your company's 4^th level of defense and reside behind your clustering devices, your firewalls, and your border routers, which are responsible for security and filtering traffic at the perimeter level. In this chapter, we'll focus on IIS 5.0 security.

## Application-Layer Firewall

A convergence of the attributes of a network firewall and an Intrusion Detection System (IDS), into a web application protocol firewall that provides greater web security, with the capability to monitor traffic bound for IIS and attacks that "do not follow recognized patterns" is here. Application-layer firewalls are designed to operate in layer seven of the OSI model and intrinsically control IIS (as an ISAPI) by proactively inspecting and verifying inbound and outbound data security. Web servers are protected from attacks on SSL encrypted sessions (port 443/https), unencrypted sessions (port 80/http), and other potential security breaches.

Application-layer firewalls exceed the level of security offered by traditional network-layered firewalls and Intrusion Detection Systems (IDS): They are not limited by the lack of proper filtering of specific web attacks, or can only detect attacks based on known signatures, as its primary criteria for blocking patterns from intruders. An Application-layer firewall is tightly integrated into your web server to achieve greater security by embedding itself into IIS through ISAPI and using many security filters, as opposed to a single static database of signatures that requires updating on a regular basis.

The key to security is to implement and maintain layered security on an ongoing basis, by addressing all of the potential threats against any of the layers of the OSI model, while preserving critical application functionality and IIS-related dependencies, essential for web servers to deliver your services and products securely. Whether using the Internet to link customers with your products, a Virtual Private Network (VPN) to link trusted vendors with your solutions, or a private Wide Area Network (WAN) to link employees with your sites and servers, security is crucial to protect your company's data from all of the above. There's no guarantee that your servers won't get hacked, but you can take steps today to build a fortified fortress and take a defensive posture and become a bastion against hackers.

Your security plan must take into consideration and address attacks against your web servers that are susceptible beyond the more common exploits. You will need to defend IIS from the following attack types, such as: Directory traversals, which exists when a hacker invokes special symbols and/or characters to escape from the root folder in an attempt to access files stored in other folders resident on your web server. Buffer overflows, which exists when a hacker persistently sends data to your servers that exceeds the buffer or maximum size permitted with each connection. Parsing attacks, which exists when a hacker modifies a string and attempts to change a value and execute a command remotely on your web server.

Having an effective security policy in place and properly configured access control lists (ACLs), are essential to the fundamentals of network security. Read chapter 2 (Router and Firewall Security) on how to secure your perimeter network.

## Understanding ISAPI Filters

Internet Server Application Programming Interface (ISAPI) filters modify the default response of your IIS server, how the web server handles web events triggered by HTTP requests, and how IIS handles URL mapping requests. In addition, you can use filters to monitor HTTP transactions, implement authentication, logging, and to support compression. Your company may require further customization of IIS and to write their own ISAPI filters. At a minimum, install a filter that uses the data structure "HTTP_FILTER_ACCESS_DENIED", which IIS points to, to handle the event started by the access denied message. Your filter must register for "SF_NOTIFY_ACCESS_DENIED" event.

By default, Microsoft doesn't load any Site-level ISAPI filters after an IIS 5 installation, unless you have also installed Exchange Server (which I don't recommend on the same machine), in which case, you will notice the "Microsoft Exchange Web Component" filter or exchfilt.dll is loaded and set to low priority. A Filter is DLL that runs in the server process level, which you link to a particular event that is activated by an HTTP request.

In the Master level (active for all websites), you will notice four filters installed and loaded (out of roughly 24 native filters):

Sspifilt.dll: Secure Socket Layer (SSL) support. This filter is set to high priority and is invoked first, if found. Remove this filter and DLL if you don't plan to use SSL (port 443) on all of the websites hosted on your web server. Don't remove this filter if you are hosting multiples websites on your web server and SSL will be required on at least one website. This filter works only at the Master level and therefore deleting it would remove SSL support for all of the websites.

Compfilt.dll: HTTP compression support. This filter is also set to high priority and is invoked second, if found. Remove this filter and DLL if you don't plan to use the compression feature of IIS.

Md5filt.dll: Digest Authentication Encryption support. This filter is set to low priority and is invoked third, if found. Remove this filter and DLL if your web server is isolated from an Active Directory server configure for this type of authentication.

Fpexedll.dll: FrontPage support. This filter is also set to low priority and is invoked fourth, if found. Remove this filter and DLL if you don't plan to support compatibility for FrontPage.

Monitor your filters periodically and check for the green up-arrows as a healthy indicator that the DLLs are properly loaded and working. Filters are loaded beginning with the first DLL in the list.

Have you implemented an IIS application protocol firewall for your web server? Although ISAPI filters (e.g., URLScan security tool) provide additional protection at the IIS level, they are not a substitute for a web application protocol firewall. Let's take a closer look at web server security through filters and with an application-layer firewall running.

No doubt, ISAPI filters offer greater control at the IIS level to strengthen your web server security. Take advantage of the power of security filters to customize and solidify your IIS server. You may have heard that the infamous URLScan filter blocked more than an attack from Nimda or CodeRed, but, when properly configured, you can benefit from a more secured, yet operational IIS server. The key is to balance and test your web application requirements and IIS-related dependencies, with the appropriate amount of security to operate a secured and functional website.

Although, we have covered some of the settings included in URLScan in this series, and these settings are also available in the Metabase, it makes sense to acknowledge the IIS Lockdown Wizard and URLScan as power weapons for your security arsenal. The ultimate security (in my opinion) though is found in knowing and understanding each parameter that makes up the Metabase.

Taking a manual approach to address the intricate components of IIS, will provide you with the underlying details you need to build a comprehensive knowledge base.

When was the last time that you updated your URLScan filter (urlscan.dll)? The current version is 2.5 and offers several features over the previous versions. Have you replaced your URLScan with URLScan-SRP, which restricts uploads to your IIS server to 30Mbytes and blocks chunked encoding transfers? If you haven't installed URLScan, begin by downloading the IIS Lockdown Wizard today, which includes version 2.0 of URLScan. The Wizard is available at this link: http://www.microsoft.com/Downloads/Release.asp?ReleaseID=43955.

Once you have installed version URLScan 2.0, upgrade it to version 2.5: http://www.microsoft.com/technet/treeview/default.asp?url=/technet/security/tools/tools/urlscan.asp

## Administration Web Site

By now you should know that I do not recommend (under any circumstances, https or not) connecting over the Internet to any internal servers or routers for administration or troubleshooting purposes. Instead, set up a private VPN connection to your internal network and then from a trusted host, establish your session(s) and carry out your tasks.

Let's begin by disabling and removing the Administration web site. Right-click on administration site and then stop the service. Next, remove the application listed in the Application Name field on the Home Directory tab in Properties. Change Execute Permission to None, remove Read, Log visits, and Index this resource. Then, replace the existing path of the Administration web site with a temporary path (e.g., c:\pm3t). (We'll change the path of your live website later in this chapter.) You will notice that any attempts to connect to the administration web site on default port 3061 will render an HTTP 403.2 (Forbidden) error or "The page cannot be displayed" message. You will get this message even if you start the administration web site.

Deselect "Enable Default Document" from the Documents tab. Go to the inetsrv folder (found in \winnt\system32) and delete the iisadmin and iisadmpwd (basically, any folder with *adm*). In IIS (via MMC), delete the iisadm and iishelp folders in the Administration Web Site, which is now just an emtpy site in "stopped" mode.

Test browsing to your default web site to make sure that the site is still operational. Delete IISADMIN and then delete IISHELP and IISSamples after you remove the folders located in \winnt\help\iishelp and \inetpub\iissamples, respectively. You will need to stop the World Wide Web Publishing service in order to delete the iishelp folder. Remove the AdminScripts folder from the inetpub folder.

If you have a public web server, consider using remote control software (with session encryption, source IP address filtering, NT authentication, and the option to change the TCP/IP port) instead of using IIS Administration. Further secure your public web server by locking down all other ports to that server in your border router ACL.

Enable TCP/IP or IPSec filtering in your Windows 2000 server. In addition, you can specify in the remote control software and the router the source IP address that will be permitted to access your web server(s). When selecting a remote control package, go with one that is not the most popular program—your network doesn't need that kind of attention (hint, hint).

| Security Tips |
| --- |
| • Replace Local Path |
| • Check dependencies |
| • Know Write permissions |

Replace the default Local Path of IIS on the Home Directory tab to a unique path. Make sure you check any dependencies (including your company's software) to the existing path before using the new path.

Avoid granting the Write permission to your site; if you must grant it, then limit this to a single subfolder that is isolated from your main site. Make sure you log any write activities performed in any of your documents.

Some companies require the use of a public FTP server to enable users to download and/or upload files. If you must use FTP server for file transmission on your web site, consider installing a dedicated server and using unique ports rather than the default ports of 20 (data) and 21 (control). Off course, you will need to implement the appropriate level of folder and file permissions.

Define a process that requires users to register (make sure you record their IP address, host name, etc.) with your company in order to use FTP services. Once they meet your criteria, provide them with your unique FTP ports. Not only will your process minimize misuse of FTP services, but also require more effort on the part of a hacker. Consider changing FTP ports on a monthly basis.

Keep in mind that users (including hackers) will need to update their client FTP ports defined in the c:\winnt\system32\drivers\etc\services or c:\windows\services file (depending on the user's operating system) every time you change your FTP server's port. Remember to update your router's ACL and firewall's policy to reflect your unique TCP/IP (and UDP) ports.

## IIS is NOT an FTP service

Don't even think about running FTP services on your web server, especially a private web server with Internet connectivity. Instead, set up a dedicated FTP server with security protection beginning in your perimeter router and firewall. Confirm that the FTP service is not running on your web server. Stop the service (and any other unnecessary service) and set to manual state if running.

Make sure that you update the ACL on your router and firewall policy to only permit non-default FTP ports through to your dedicated FTP server(s). Block all the other TCP/IP ports and set a maximum connection limitation in your static route (or address translation entry) to your FTP server. Avoid using unlimited values for your maximum connections.

An often-overlooked area is the restriction of IP address at the IIS server level. This is usually because if you have a public web server, you typically want everyone to be able to visit your website(s). Therefore, the default setting of "All computers will be granted access" is accepted and never revisited to exclude IP addresses that you don't want to access your website.

Relying on Windows 2000 IP filtering is no excuse for not reinforcing security at the IIS level or in your border router and firewall. You will need to enable IP filtering in your border routers, firewalls, clustering devices, and all of your servers.

As soon as you discover from your logs IP addresses attempting to access your perimeter, exclude these addresses from accessing your IIS server. Off course, you can also check around for sites that offer a list of "offending IP addresses" and take a proactive approach toward securing your network!

| What if? |
| --- |
| • Master of security? |
| • Candidate for Murphy? |
| • Network a parking lot? |

Are you the master of network security in your company or a candidate of Murphy's Law? Is your network the destination address of ongoing security or a parking lot for a hacker convention? When was the last time you maintain security?

If your security is configured the wrong way, expect hackers to experiment with your network and Mr. Murphy to pay you a visit and test your "human acceleration tolerance".

Are you willing to sacrifice some server acceleration for more security? Imagine if you could keep a hacker from defacing your website, no matter how hard they tried [period]. It's possible to achieve more network security, while maintaining an acceptable level of server performance, see what I call, Medina's Read-Only Content (ROC) approach below.

When was the last time a hacker wrote to a read-only CD-ROM?

## Medina's Read-Only Content (ROC) Approach

If your website consists of mostly static pages and your web server has a fast DVD or CD-ROM drive, record a CD-ROM with a complete build of your website structure. Go to the Home Directory tab to specify the location of your recorded content and then the Documents tab to specify your default document.

For example, to test this, I used Microsoft's Office CD "MSOFFSBE9" and the path with default.htm as the document:

"d:\pfiles\common\msshared\websrvex\04\serk\1033\"

Make sure you clear your browser's cache before testing.

A slightly different approach is to continue using your local drive with a copy of your original website files available in your web server's DVD or CD-ROM drive. Use a file copy program with synchronization and scheduling capabilities to compare your live website files (stored on your local drive) with the original files (stored on your CD-ROM). Schedule file-checks using 5-minute intervals and if necessary, replace any compromised/modified file with its original file version.

If you anticipate content updates on a regular basis, consider either excluding these files from your file checks or updating your original website image on a regular basis, which can be used as part of your company's disaster recovery planning.

Both approach can be accomplished without using Windows sharing or IIS web sharing. If you choose to use the first approach, consider increasing your CD-ROM cache and/or adding additional CD-ROM drives to handle your website traffic load, if necessary.

Now that you are familiar with what I call Medina's ROC approach, let's go over some basic steps with a look at Execute Permissions and Application Protection of your default web site.

Avoid using the "Scripts and Executables" permission for your web site; make sure that execute permissions is set to "Scripts only" to prevent a hacker from using the execute permission against you.

Avoid using "Medium (Pooled)" for your protection level; make sure that application protection is set to "High (Isolated)" level. This is the highest level of operating system protection against a malfunctioning application.

Are your web servers mapping unnecessary extensions and caching unwanted DLLs? When was the last time you modified Microsoft's default list of extension mappings and HTTP actions?

## Extension Mappings

Upon installing IIS and a quick view of the Applications Mappings in the Configuration button on the Home Directory tab, you will noticed that "Cache ISAPI applications" is enabled, by default. Below, you will find a list of extensions (that is, DLLs) configured to be pre-loaded to improve the performance of your web server by caching future page requests (e.g., index.asp).

## The Problem

The problem with keeping Microsoft's default extension mappings is that DLLs used in extension mappings can potentially circumvent security through an existing or future vulnerability in the Internet Server Application Programming Interface (ISAPI) extension (e.g., msw3prt.dll used by printer extension, accepts input, and allows printing via HTTP).

Ask yourself if you are:

1. Utilizing the minimum extensions required for your web servers to operate?
2. Overlooking a security compromise by not minimizing the use of DLLs?
3. Accepting Microsoft's generic values for your production server security?
4. Defeating the purpose of improving performance by caching unused DLLs?

As you ponder these questions, remember not to underestimate a hacker's determination to compromise your server or network security.

Before making modifications to your live network, make sure you have a successful backup of each server and to test your changes before updating a live environment.

## The Solution

Consider reviewing the mapping list below, remove unnecessary extensions/DLLs, change the default executable path of DLLs, set the appropriate HTTP actions (avoid your application receiving all requests from users), and minimize the use of script actions (write permission).

Keep in mind, that DLLs defined in the mapping extensions can circumvent security through a bug in Internet Server Application Programming Interface (ISAPI), which can assist a hacker (e.g., unchecked buffer that can lead to local system privileges) with an attack on your server.

## Extension Mapping List

GHP = Get, Head, Post
GHPT = Get, Head, Post, Trace
GP = Get, Post
OGHPPDT = Options, Get, Head, Post, Put, Delete, Trace

| Extension | Dependency | DLL | HTTP Action |
|---|---|---|---|
| .htw | Used by Index Server | webhits.dll | GHP |
| .ida | Used by Index Server | idq.dll | GHP |
| .idq | Used by Index Server | idq.dll | GHP |
| .asp | Used by ASP for script handling | asp.dll | GHPT |
| .cer | Used by ASP for certificate request | asp.dll | GHPT |
| .cdx | Used by ASP for index files | asp.dll | GHPT |
| .asa | Used by ASP for example for globa.asa | asp.dll | GHPT |
| .htr | Used by IIS for resetting password | ism.dll | GP |
| .idc | Used by IIS for ODBC connections | httpodbc.dll | OGHPPDT |
| .shtm | Used by IIS for Server-side include | ssinc.dll | GP |
| .shtml | Used by IIS for Server-side include | ssinc.dll | GP |
| .stm | Used by IIS for Server-side include | ssinc.dll | GP |
| .printer | Used by IIS for web printing | msw3prt.dll | GP |

Modify and test your IIS session timeout (default 20 minutes) and ASP Script timeout (default 90 seconds) and use realistic values that reflect your web environment. Disable buffering and parent paths.

Modify and test the number of script engines (default 125), the number of ASP file cached (default 250), and CGI script timeout (default 300 seconds), again to reflect your web environment. Enable unsuccessful client requests to event log.

Select "Do not cache ASP files" if you are not supporting ASP scripting on your web server.

| Streaming Server |
| --- |
| • Streaming Media Server<br>• Media Services<br>• Authentication Package |

The e-volution of the Internet as the new messenger of our civilization—the electronic carrier of our communications and global marketplace for the $21^{st}$ century, provides the infrastructure to enable businesses to host live web events across the world.

## Streaming Media Server

Like with any new networking technology, servers—as well as services such as streaming media—need to be secured when privacy is a prerequisite or confidentiality cannot be compromised. Windows Media Services (WMS) is Microsoft's solution to stream live or stored multimedia (audio and video) content over the Internet. Although your company may be outsourcing streaming media now, we will address securing WMS to assist you with security, in the event IT budget constraints require that your IT group manage this service later.

## Windows Media Services

To set up your Streaming Media Server, launch the "Windows 2000 Configure Your Server" found in Administrative Tools, click on Streaming Media Server listed below Web/Media Server, then click on Start to begin the Windows Media Services installation using the Windows Components Wizard. A quick look at Windows 2000 Services once installation is complete will show that ".\NetShowService" is the default startup account used for each of the four services (nsmonitor, nsprogram, nsstation, and nsunicast) with the executable path set to the \Windows Media\Server subfolder in the System32 folder.

As you can see, the setup wizard used a default path for the executables, which is common knowledge with hackers and the first place they will most likely search. (One day, Microsoft will update their setup interface and provide an option to specify a unique path in ALL of their applications.) Let's take a step back and talk about the server and the file system you should use:

First, you will want to set up a dedicated server and file system with the directory structure for unicast publishing points on a separate disk drive to stream your media. Second, you will want to replace the startup account ".\NetShowService" with the System account (security context). Third, you will want to rename the publishing point directory to a unique name and set proper directory permissions. Off course, you will need to address security using the layered approach for an effective defensive posture.

Launch the Windows Media Administrator program and confirm that "Connected to <your server>" is displayed on the bottom left side of your windowpane. Set the maximum unicast clients, streaming bandwidth, and the media player file bitrate in the General tab of Server Properties to realistic values other than the default of "No Limit". It's important that you understand the performance peak or load capacity of your server beforehand to avoid unexpected server behavior when stressed to the limit.

# Authentication Package

Control the release of media streaming by enforcing authentication and requiring a login ID and password in order for unicast users to receive live or stored content. At a minimum, use the HTTP and NTLM Account Database with Access Control List (ACL) checking for your authentication package in the Publishing Point Security tab. Avoid using distribution authentication to distribute streams to other servers. If your company must use this, then consider changing the proxy password weekly. Set logging period to daily and change the default log file directory to a unique directory in another location.

Avoid using HTTP streaming over port 80 to support users with media player behind a firewall. If your company must support HTTP streaming, then consider enabling it as needed. Make sure your border router is filtering traffic to this server. Replace the default publishing point path <ASFRoot> for Unicast On-Demand with a unique directory and set maximum limit for clients and bandwidth in the Unicast Publishing Point screen of Configure Server. Avoid using file transfers. If your company requires FTS, then specify the IP address, TTL, and enable logging.

| Security Tips |
| --- |
| • Use HTTP & NTLM DB |
| • Avoid HTTP streaming |
| • Change publishing points and logging path |

At a minimum, use the HTTP and NTLM Account Database with Access Control List (ACL) to require login ID & password. Avoid HTTP streaming over port 80; if you must support this for your users (behind firewall), enable only as necessary. Change publishing points instead of using ASFRoot.

By default, your media streaming server monitors Client Events, Server Events, Admin Events, and Alert events with the maximum buffer size set to 200. I suggest you increase this buffer size from 200 to 400.

## "WMTPerf" Monitor

You will have to enable client monitoring to view client connections and check for repetitive IP addresses or suspicious attempts to your server. Make sure that you closely monitor your logs and connections regularly. In the executable path of \Windows Media\Server in the System32 folder, you will find a Microsoft Common Console Document named "wmtperf", which will provide you with the defined media streaming objects and counters to monitor performance statistics. You will also find two .bat files (stopns and startns) with the following order to stop and start the media server:

Stopns:
net stop nsmonitor /y
net stop nsprogram /y
net stop nsstation /y
net stop nsunicast /y

Startns:
net start nsunicast
net start nsstation
net start nsprogram
net start nsmonitor

If your streaming server is being used inside an Intranet only, change the default port of 7007/1755 to a unique port and the authentication package to Windows NT LAN Manager and Account Database. If you are using Windows Media Encoder to create live or stored media, consider changing the default port of 1792 (MSBD) and 1793 (HTTP) to a unique port for each. The objective is to make it difficult for hackers to break into your server. Consider changing default ports for internal servers and hosts whenever possible. Changing default ports for public servers may not be feasible since it would require that all of your clients also change their ports in order to connect to your server.

Operating system and application security is a prerequisite if you want to effectively apply security using the OSI Model layer approach. When thinking of web server security, you need to consider securing the underlying layer (that is, the operating system—in this case, Windows 2000). Make sure that you stop and set to manual state any unnecessary service your server is running and configure TCP/IP filtering. Take time to understand and document your Windows 2000 Server security baseline to maintain consistency with future server builds or installations. Know your configuration and test each service before changing its state to disable.

See chapter three (Windows 2000 Server Security) for information on how to secure your operating system.

# Chapter 5

# ─ SQL 2000 Server Security

## Database Server Security

- Mutually exclusive
- Relative frequency
- Collectively exhaustive
- Store & monitor log files
- Security audit trace
- Authentication mode
- Data Sources
- Enterprise Manager
- Security logins
- Server role
- Database role
- The triple threat
- 4-R rule of administration
- What if it's true?

Will you be another statistic? Is the connection to your database server mutually exclusive? Has database security become an empirical concept among database administrators in your company? If the probability of an attack in the future is determined by your observations of security threats in the past, how do you know that your server is not being hacked right now?

Toss a quarter and what do you get? Obviously, you'll have a 50% percent chance that it will be heads and a 50% chance it will be tails. Is the security of your network left to chance? Are you vulnerable to a breed of vipers that slither in and out of your network, ready to attack?

See chapter three (Windows 2000 Security) to implement operating system security before proceeding with SQL 2000 security.

## Mutually Exclusive

It's important that you have a thorough understanding of your company's application requirements and external dependencies to the database server(s) before you begin the process of securing your database and the data. Your SQL server should not be running IIS or another web application. The reason why you don't want IIS on the same server is for the obvious inherent security issues that exist with port 80; for example, why set up your database server to distribute the automation of a WORM on your network from other IIS servers behind your firewall? If your SQL server is also running IIS, it's possible that whoever set up IIS on your database server is also running FTP service, by default. Although your SQL server is behind a production or corporate firewall, it doesn't justify running unnecessary applications or services.

It is crucial that SQL runs on a dedicated server with no other applications or services, such as IIS (Internet Information Server) or FTP (File Transfer Protocol). Failure to run in "dedicated mode" will open up additional ports or sockets and put your database server security at risk. Whether you're running SQL on Windows 2000 or Oracle on Unix, the operating system—by default—starts unnecessary services or processes that open up additional TCP/IP ports; these non-database specific ports must be stopped and permanently disabled.

Front-end communications to your database server must be mutually exclusive over a non-default specified TCP/IP port. Prevent your database server from responding to broadcast requests from clients and force protocol encryption to protect confidential data from being viewed by users.

The *Default Port, Force Protocol Encryption*, and *Hide Server* option can be set in the SQL 2000 Server Network Utility. Be prepared to restart the MSSQL$<Instance name> service for changes to take effect.

Schedule a meeting with your IT manager to review the existing configuration of your SQL server before applying security. You'd be surprised by what you and others will learn when you go beyond the surface level of your database server configuration.

## Relative Frequency

Is a hacker about to run the code of his or her choice against your database server again? Microsoft reported another security vulnerability (Q326573) that affects MDAC versions 2.5, 2.6 and 2.7. A patch (see MS02-040) is available to fix the "Unchecked buffer in MDAC function that could enable a SQL server compromise" with above versions.

The (above) vulnerability has a moderate rating, but is the security level of your database server moderate? How secure are your IIS servers? Have you implemented security (in other words, a router with ACL) between your Web servers and your database server?

Your SQL Instance name should be a unique name and not the default name of your server. Before changing the SQL default port, verify that your custom application is not statically coded to communicate with SQL on port 1433 only—in other words, check for any dependencies to port 1433. Specify a custom destination path for SQL Program Files and SQL Data Files.

| Security Tips |
| --- |
| • Do not use default path |
| • Restrict access to data |
| • Configure MDAC |

Do not use the default installation path of %localdrive% Program FilesMicrosoft SQL Server, because this is a predictable path (just like winnt) and hackers already know it.

Restrict access to your database server and configure Microsoft Data Access Component (MDAC) on required front-end servers only. (We'll address changing the winnt path later in the series. Right now, your database security is top priority.)

## Collectively Exhaustive

Just as a server that lacks the appropriate service pack and hotfixes is a target for hackers, an improperly configured server is equally vulnerable to an outside or inside attack. Your SQL server is no exception, just more challenging for hackers. Your database server, and especially your production servers should not use *Client for Microsoft or File and Print Sharing* services at the O/S level—even if the servers are protected by a hardware or UNIX-based firewall.

Make sure you disable *NetBios over TCP, LMHOST Lookup,* and do not register your database server connection's address in DNS; use the invalid IP address of the server instead. Disable all of the Windows 2000 services except for the following: Event Log, MSSQL$<Instance Name>, Plug and Play, Security Accounts Manager and SQLAgent$ <Instance Name>.

Remember to perform a full backup of your server before changing the state of the server.

Make sure that you change the services from automatic to manual mode first, then clear the event log, reboot the server, and test connectivity from your application and SQL Client to your database. Once you have confirmed that your server is properly working and there are no critical events in the event log, change the services from manual to disabled state.

| Security Tips |
| --- |
| • Stop unwanted services<br>• Set to manual mode<br>• Change hexadecimal |

Stop unwanted services and set to manual mode first. In the event that you have to change a service in disable mode to automatic mode, and you cannot, go to Hive key in the Registry.

Change the hexadecimal number in the Value Data field from 4 to 2 of the REG_DWORD "Start" of the Hive key:

HKEY_LOCAL_MACHINESYSTEMCurrentControlSetServices
When was the last time you applied a SQL service pack or hotfix? Or updated the version of MDAC drivers on your Web servers and on your database server?

You need to understand one thing when it comes to network security—if you don't identify and isolate the weak links in your network security, a hacker will! It's only a matter of time before someone finds out how to exploit your system. When was the last time you consistently stored and monitored your log files off-site?

# Store and Monitor Your Log Files Off-Site

Put a mechanism in place to move, without using IPC, your production server log files off-site to a central repository location (or server). By doing this, you will limit the hacker's ability to remove any evidence (or footprints) recorded in your log files. A better solution would be to set up your events or audits to report automatically to an off-site server and then immediately rename the log files.

Failure to consistently store and monitor your log files off-site will provide the hacker unlimited time to clear his steps. This tip applies especially to your production network logs (such as those for your perimeter router, firewall, servers, and load balancing and cluster devices).

# Security Audit Trace Template

Let's begin by creating a security audit trace template with a list of security events to monitor on your SQL 2000 server. In Profiler, go to File+New+Trace Template and log in. Go to the Events tab and add Security Audit, Sessions and Objects to list of event classes (in the pane on the right).

Below is a sample list of the events you should consider monitoring when defining your security audit template:

Logs creation or deletion of database users:
Audit Add DB User Event

Creation or deletion of log-in to server role:
Audit Add Login to Server Role Event

Creation or deletion of member to database role:
Audit Add Member to DB Role Event

Logs audit changes:
Audit Change Audit Event

Logs SQL log-in password changes
Audit Login Change Password Event

Logs client log-in attempts:
Audit Login Failed

Logs Grant, Deny and Revoke (GDR) Windows log-in rights:
Audit Login GDR Event

Logs Grant, Deny and Revoke object permissions:
Audit Object GDR Event
Logs start, pause and shutdown activities:
Audit Server Starts and Stops

Logs Grant, Deny and Revoke statement permissions:
Audit Statement GDR Event

Logs users connected to server:
ExistingConnections

Logs the object accessed (select, insert, delete):
Objects\Objects:Created

Logs the deletion (drop index, drop table) of an object:
Objects\Objects:Deleted

After adding the above events, go to the Data Columns tab and add DBUserName, LoginName, Permissions, TargetLoginName and TargetUserName; then go to the General tab, click on Save As, and assign a name (for example, s3c-aud1t-t3mp) for your template and store in a custom path. Now you are ready to create a trace file with your new custom template and save it to either a file or database table.

Although my preference is to save the trace (audits) to a file and then transfer the file to an off-site server every 10 minutes, saving to a database table will work too. However, a table-based solution—for example, populating a table, scheduling a dump and moving the dump—will require more effort than a file-based solution, not to mention that using a file will consume less T1 bandwidth and require less time to transfer off-site.

| Security Tips |
| --- |
| • DB password protection<br>• Choose the right authentication mode |

As the database administrator, you must guard your database passwords from becoming common knowledge with network administrators.

This task will be difficult to achieve if you decide to use Windows Authentication Mode, because the account name and password will not be stored on the database server side.

## Authentication Mode

During SQL 2000 setup, Windows Authentication Mode is the default choice. This mode is recommended by Microsoft because it supports trusted (relies on authentication at the AD or Domain level) connections between the client and the database server. Mixed Mode—AKA SQL authentication—supports non-trusted connections; that is, the log-in name and password are stored locally on the database server and a connection from a non-trusted client will be accepted, as long as the correct account name and password is provided.

If you choose Mixed Mode, you will also notice that the password for the SA account is optional. Regardless of which mode you choose, you will need to set a unique password for the SA account. My preference is to use SQL authentication. I'll explain why: The problem I see with using Windows Authentication Mode is that if—or when—a hacker obtains your domain administrator password, he or she will also have access to your database server and your tables. In the meantime, the database passwords may be common knowledge and shared among network administrators. I suggest that this password be limited to a primary and secondary DBA. Therefore, I prefer the extra level of protection by enforcing a separate complicated password for the SA account, one that is not shared with network administrators, to avoid the "too many hands in the cookie jar" syndrome. Depending on your environment, you may choose to go with SQL authentication instead of Windows authentication.

| Security Tips |
| --- |
| • Intermediary security<br>• Secure front-end<br>• Secure back-end<br>• Secure connection<br>• Protect your databases |

The main advantage of Windows Authentication Mode is that only authenticated clients can establish a trusted connection to your database. But, the mode is not designed to protect your database server, as would the installation of a second firewall, or a router with appropriate ACL.

The absence of an intermediary security device between your clients and database server is an overlooked security area that should be addressed by your database administrator and IT staff, sooner rather than later. In the absence of security, there's an opportunity for intrusion.

## Data Sources

Creating a User or System DSN in Microsoft ODBC Administrator on your Web servers is a straightforward process. The important thing here is to configure, in Client Configuration, each DSN with TCP and the non-default port of your database server (other than port 1433) and enter the appropriate account name and password. Make sure you are using the most stable and secured version of MDAC and record the version number (see About). Select the box "Change the default database to" and enter your database name.

If you want to test your access to your database server using Microsoft's NorthWind database, select it form the list of databases and enter the password for the SA account. If you are using NamedPipes, your client will require an IPC connection to the database server, which I don't recommend for security reasons.

| Security Tips |
| :---: |
| • Avoid unlimited users |
| • Set realistic values |
| • Understand capacity |
| • Benchmark performance |

The most overlooked setting is the Maximum Concurrent User Connections. The default value of zero represents unlimited connections. The problem is that your database server most likely can't handle unlimited user connections.

If a hacker (or erratic procedure) managed to initiate an abnormal amount of connections and/or traffic, it would overload your database server and potentially by-pass database security and render your database useless.

Accepting unlimited connections also implies that your staff does not have a proper understanding or realistic estimation about the existing capacity or future expectations of customers and user connections. The goal is to secure your server using realistic values and not with default values, which often defeat the purpose of having security in the first place.

Performance benchmarks of your existing application should provide the statistics you need to determine the maximum number of user connections that your database server can reliably handle.

## Enterprise Manager

Select Properties for your database server listed in SQL Server Group in Enterprise Manager. Go to the Security tab and set Failure on Audit level to record failed log-in attempts; then go to the Connections tab and disable Remote Server Connections, which by default allows other SQL servers to connect via Remote Procedure Call (RPC) to your database server. Enter a value in Maximum Concurrent User Connections and don't accept the default unlimited value. Go to Server Settings tab and select the appropriate behavior of your server, then go to the Active Directory tab and add the instance, if you elect to integrate SQL with AD.

Below is the second part of my SQL Security Checklist. In my third part of the "Protect your database server" mini-series, we will focus on role-based security, SID and GUID, permissions and delegation.

| Security Tips |
| --- |
| • Take a holistic view |
| • Security life cycle |
| • Create security project |
| • Lead better security |
| • Avoid Triple Threat |

Is your company taking a holistic view of network security, or is it too deep in the trenches—and constrained by the economic downturn—to see the big picture?

Is the security life cycle of your database server(s) about to expire?

Will you take the initiative to create a security project, lead the esprit de corps to enforce better security and avoid what I call the triple threat? In the absence of security, there exists an opportunity for network intrusion.

When was the last time you checked your database server security? Have you installed the latest cumulative patch (Q316333) for SQL Server 2000, MS02-056?

## Security Logins

Let's continue by reviewing the security login accounts that exist in your database server. (The Security Login folder is accessible in the Enterprise Manager and is part of the SQL Server Registration Group.) You will notice the active login accounts (in the pane on the right), once you de-collapse the Security folder and click on Logins. Now is the time to thoroughly examine the list of login accounts and verify the need for—and the type of—database access level.

Avoid unnecessary database access to your server by removing obsolete or unused accounts. If an account is required, verify the user's role and grant access only to the database tables required to achieve the business objective. It is vitally important that you change the default database (Master) specified for the login account used via MDAC/ODBC from front-end web servers; failure to change this default database will result in a server compromise.

Change the default database assigned to new login accounts, especially for the login accounts that are used via MDAC/ODBC connections from your front-end Web servers. Also, avoid putting any passwords in the Registry where they will be accessible to others and become common knowledge. (I've witnessed environments where the password is defined in a String Value in the Registry and available to anyone remotely.)

## Server Role

To change the default database, assign server role(s), and define the database access, select the login account and double-click on it. Find the Defaults section and "Specify the default language and database for this login" in the General tab, which is displayed in the Properties box of the login you selected. Next, go to the Server Roles tab and—with caution—assign the appropriate role to grant security privileges for the user.

Keep in mind that access granted at the Server Role level is propagated throughout the database scheme. In other words, you're assigning privileges that have system-wide ramifications and can put the integrity of your SQL Server at risk. Take extra precaution when assigning the role of system administrators, as this role rules over all the other (security, server, setup, process, disk, and bulk-insert) administrative roles and the database creator role.

| Security Tips |
|---|
| • Replace BUILTIN accts. |
| • Avoid inherent issues |
| • Know the admin roles |

Replace the BUILTIN administrators group with the individual login names to avoid an inherent security issue later due to an overlooked member of the built-in group.

Take note of the fact that other administrative roles (for example, process and server) have the kill and/or shutdown privileges, similar to the system administrator's role. Next, click on the Database Access tab and prepare to add or remove the appropriate database(s) necessary for each account.

Your database server should only include the databases of your company and not sample databases, such as Northwind. Make sure that you have a full backup before removing any databases or making changes to a production server. Always make sure that you have a safety net to fall back on, especially when working in a production environment and when time is of the essence (which is also the case in most corporate environments).

## Database Role

Database Access allows you to set the role for each database that you previously assigned to a login account. Depending on your work situation, you may implement the application role (with set password) instead of the standard role typically used. Although you cannot modify the special database role Public (which is similar to the Guest account in NT) or drop its members, you can restrict users from being the "db_owner" or from being other roles (for example, db_accessadmin, db_securityadmin, db_datawriter, and so forth).

## The Triple Threat

The triple threat is not a new group of hackers (at least to my knowledge) or a set of new hacking tools—yet it can hurt your organization and/or your career! If you recall, in the beginning of this chapter, I asked, "Is your company taking a holistic view of network security...?" and "Is the security life cycle of your database server(s) about to expire...?" Security is our weapon against a hacking culture that thrives on creating chaos across a connected world of computer villages. Lack of security is an open invitation to hackers everywhere to take ownership of your data and, ultimately, your network. The triple threat is target, time and cost:

- **Target goal:** What are you trying to accomplish?
  You need to see the big picture to know how much network security is needed in your organization. How will you get there?
- **Time goal:** How long will it take to get there?
  Know how long it will take to implement network security. If security is a moving target, then when will the implementation of security be complete?

- **Cost goal:** How much will it cost to get there?
  Know how much it will cost to maintain network security. How much are you willing to spend to recover from a network attack? Will you maintain your security life cycle?

In short, project management might be an option for you, but security is not. The greatest security threat to your organization begins when you have an understanding of the security vulnerabilities that exist but you do not do anything about them. Having a short-term security plan or taking a passive role will eventually assist an attack on your network.

## SQL 2000 Server Security Checklist

1. Use a custom installation path for SQL program files and SQL data files.
2. Change the default TCP/IP (1433) port for SQL connections.
3. Implement security between your front-end servers and the database server.
4. Restrict access to your database server to front-end servers that require a connection.
5. Block all TCP/IP and UDP ports except for the SQL port you plan to use.
6. Disable unnecessary O/S services and processes; uninstall non-SQL programs.
7. Apply TCP/IP filtering in the O/S level and only accept your SQL port.
8. Make sure that you are running the most stable and secure MDAC version and patch/hotfix.
9. Disable unnecessary SQL network libraries, components and agents.

10. Confirm server role is SQL only and do not run IIS on the same server.
11. Customize Auto Start SQL Service and Agent to use local System Account.
12. Use Mixed Mode for Authentication Mode and set unique password for SA account.
13. Apply service packs and hotfixes at O/S and SQL level.
14. Restrict Enterprise Manager access.
15. Implement a mechanism to automatically store production log files off-site without using IPC connections.
16. Monitor your log files on a daily basis for suspicious or failed attempts.
17. Don't settle for unlimited default values for present and near-future connections; specify a realistic number.
18. Implement intermediary security (I can't emphasize this enough) between your clients and database server.
19. Carefully consider which authentication mode is appropriate for your environment. If you are the DBA or a network administrator, the decision is simple.
20. Assign another database to new logins other than the default Master database.

Did you pass the test? Does your SQL server configuration already include the security tips in this chapter? If yes, kudos! It's been my experience that some of these basic steps have often been overlooked by experienced IT professionals. If you're serious about security, you must pay attention to details and leave no room for hackers.

The purpose of my book is to explore the various areas in your network and bring to the surface any security vulnerabilities that have been overlooked. The intention of this chapter is not to tell you how to set up a database server, but to point out the areas you should be aware of when configuring a SQL 2000 Server.

## What If It's True?

What if it's true that hackers roam the Internet like roaring lions seeking to devour your confidential data? Will you be steadfast in the allegiance of network security or surrender to the stronghold of hackers? Is security the monarch of your domain or will you end up in exile?

Despite recent high profile attacks, most businesses still lack proper security, don't have an effective security plan, and have poor security practices in place. As sophisticated and automated hacking tools are made available, hackers will have faster access to security exploits than in the history of the Internet. Since most network administrators have no previous security experience or any security training, servers are set up using out-of-the-box (default) security settings; default settings generally lack the necessary security for web sites.

Are you the Royal Administrator or Apprentice of network security in your company? Are you supporting false security or will you be thrown in the lion's den, like Daniel?

# Chapter 6

## Exchange 2000 Server Security

### Mail Server Security

- Diagnostics Logging
- Security tab
- Monitoring tab
- Protocols
- First storage group
- First routing groups
- Be first not last
- To MIME or not to MIME
- Recipient policies
- E-mail address types
- Global address security
- Inheritable permissions
- Update Service
- Outlook 2000 clients
- S/MIME
- Security Zone
- 4-R Rule of admin.
- What if it's true?

The paradigm of IT spending today is indicative of a lackluster economy in search of a business hero or savior. The shift from an exuberant market to its antithesis has left projects stranded in the desert of information technology, but is the security of your mail server real or a mirage?

Is your approach to security proactive, or an inverted reflection of a distant future? Will your IT convoy prevail, or will hackers commandeer what's left of your security and take hostage your mail server? In this chapter we will focus on securing your Exchange 2000 server.

See chapter three (Windows 2000 Security) to implement operating system security before proceeding with Exchange 2000 security.

# Diagnostics Logging

Set the logging level of each category of Exchange 2000 services listed on the Diagnostics Logging tab of your server's Properties, beneath the Servers object in the First Administrative Group. Avoid using the maximum logging level except when troubleshooting a service and when additional information will assist you in diagnosing and solving an issue. Keep in mind that the maximum level will put additional strain on your server's performance. At a minimum, consider enabling logging and testing the following levels for each service:

| Services | Category | Logging Level |
|---|---|---|
| MSExchangeIS System | Table Cache | Medium |
| | Move Mailbox | Medium |
| Public Folder | Access Control | Medium |
| | Send On Behalf Of | Medium |
| | Views | Medium |
| | Non-delivery Reports | Medium |
| Mailbox | Access Control | Medium |
| | Send On Behalf Of | Medium |
| | Local Replication | Medium |
| MSExchangeMTA | Security | Medium |
| | Directory Access | Medium |

| | | |
|---|---|---|
| MSExchangeSRS | Security | Medium |
| | Directory Access | Medium |
| MSExchangeTransport | Queuing Engine | Medium |
| | SMTP Protocol | Medium |
| POP3Svc | Authentication | Medium |
| | Content Engine | Medium |

## Security tab

Consider removing users and groups and/or modifying the existing permissions assigned in the Security tab to reflect your organizational structure. At a minimum, replace the group Everyone with Authenticated Users to prevent group from inheritable permissions. First deselect "Allow inheritable permissions from parent to propagate to this object". (This step will generate a message dialogue box asking you to either copy or remove or cancel.) Second, click on the Remove button to prevent permissions from propagating and delete the group Everyone. You will notice that other users and groups will be automatically removed from the list except for Authenticated Users. Consider creating new unique users and groups with limited members and permissions for each role and avoid using Microsoft's Built-in accounts, by default.

## Monitoring tab

By default, you will notice a resource name, "Default Microsoft Exchange Services", which is defined by Exchange to monitor the critical state (i.e., when a service is no longer running) of the following services:

- Microsoft Exchange Information Store
- Microsoft Exchange MTA Stacks
- Microsoft Exchange Routine Engine
- Microsoft Exchange System Attendant
- Simple Mail Transport Protocol (SMTP)
- World Wide Web Publishing Service

Consider adding additional services for monitoring to this resource, such as DNS Client, Event Log, Windows Time, and Alerter. Test stopping a service and then check the Monitor tab; you will find that Default Microsoft Exchange Services critical state is in stopped mode. Check details on the above service to confirm that the service reported is the one that you stopped. (I've noticed it can take several minutes after a service has stopped for the Monitor tab to report the changed state.)

Add the resource SMTP queue growth to monitor and set the minutes to 15 for warning state and 30 for critical state. You want to proactively monitor the normal and abnormal growth patterns of your SMTP queue. Next, add the resource CPU Threshold and set duration to 7 minutes, warning state to 70%, and critical state to 90% to monitor high CPU utilization. Make sure Full Text Indexing is set to low.

## Protocols

HTTP Virtual Server

If your running Exchange Virtual Server, make sure that you deselect Anonymous Access and Basic Authentication (uses clear text to send password) and use the Integrated Windows Authentication instead in the Authentication Methods button on the Access tab of Exchange object Properties. Next, deselect Directory browsing, Script source access, and carefully review whether you need to enable Write control for both the Exchange and Public objects. Finally, confirm that Execute Permissions level is properly set to reflect your Exchange Organization; when in doubt, set the permission to None, test your server functionality, then set permission accordingly.

POP3 Virtual Server

If your running POP3 Virtual Server, make sure that you limit the number of connections using a realistic value that reflects your user environment and avoid supporting unlimited connections. In the IP address box, scroll down and select your IP address instead of using "All unassigned". In the Advanced tab, you will notice the default port for POP3 and SSL port is 110 and 995, respectively. If possible, change the default POP3 port to a unique port in Exchange and in the services file of each server and user. In the Access tab, you will notice Basic authentication is selected, which sends password in clear text. Deselect this type of authentication and use the Integrated Windows Authentication instead. At a minimum and without hesitation, install and configure (require 128-bit encryption and secure channel) a Verisign server certificate to encrypt and secure your e-mail communications. Take advantage of the TCP/IP filter option in Exchange and change the default setting of computers that can access the POP3 virtual server from "All except the list below" to "Only the list below", then specify the single or subnet IP addresses of approved hosts.

SMTP Virtual Server

If your running SMTP Virtual Server, make sure that you limit the number of connections using a realistic value that reflects your user environment and avoid supporting unlimited connections. Similar to POP3 properties, in the IP address box, scroll down and select your IP address instead of using "All unassigned". Before going to the advanced tab, select Enable Logging and change the Active Log Format to ODBC Logging, if you have a dedicated logging database server and an ODBC connection defined. Click on Properties to specify the MDAC/ODBC Data Source Name (DSN), Table, User Name, and Password. See chapter five (SQL 2000 Security) for instructions on how to create and configure an ODBC connection. I recommend that you set up a separate database server to handle all of your logs with unique tables for each server type (web, mail, firewall, database, etc.). If a dedicated database server is not available for storing logging information, then temporarily use the W3C Extended Log File Format and set the following properties:

- New Log Time Period to Hourly.
- Use Local time for file naming and rollover.
- Log file directory to a unique path and file name.
- Enable Extended Logging Options for:
  - Date
  - Time
  - Client IP Address
  - User Name
  - Service Name
  - Server Name
  - Server IP Address
  - Server Port
  - Method
  - URI Query
  - Bytes Received
  - Time Taken
  - Cookie
  - Referrer

Click on the advanced tab and verify that the IP address listed is the IP of Exchange server. Next, enable filter on this IP address by clicking on Apply Filter in the Edit button. Similar to POP3 Virtual Server, in the Access tab, you will notice that Basic authentication is selected (in the Authentication button), which sends password in clear text. Deselect this type of authentication and use the Integrated Windows Authentication instead. At a minimum and without hesitation, install and configure (require 128-bit encryption and secure channel) a Verisign server certificate to encrypt and secure your e-mail communications. Take advantage of the TCP/IP filter option in Exchange and change the default setting of computers that can access the SMTP virtual server from "All except the list below" to "Only the list below", then specify the single or subnet IP addresses of approved hosts. Enforce Relay restrictions if you must relay electronic messages from other mail servers or web server running virtual SMTP. Deselect "Allow all computers which successfully authenticate to relay, regardless of the list above and specify the IP address for each server.

Enforce limits on each message and session size and limit the number of messages per connection and of recipients per message. Send a copy of Non-Delivery Reports (NDRs) to a non-Administrative mailbox and monitor NDS e-mails. Replace the Badmail directory with a unique path and file name. Forward unresolved recipient mail to your dedicated logging server. In the Delivery tab, set the following numeric values (minutes) for Outbound and Local intervals:

- First retry interval to 30 minutes.
- Second retry interval to 60 minutes.
- Third retry interval to 120 minutes.
- Subsequent retry to 240 minutes.
- Delay notification to 1 hour.
- Expiration timeout to 3 days.

- Local Delay notification to 1 hour.
- Local Expiration timeout to 3 days.

Outbound Security defaults to anonymous access to transfer messages with other mail systems. Since both anonymous and basic authentication do not provide adequate password security, consider using Integrated Windows Authentication (with limited network account) and enabling Transport Layer Security (TLS) to encrypt e-mail communications between your mail servers and with other mail systems on the Internet, whenever possible. Guard your Administrator account and password and avoid using a privileged account for authentication. Adjust outbound connections using a realistic numeric value that reflects your user environment. (Depending on your company and domain size, you will need to either decrease or increase the default numeric value of 1000 for outbound connections and 100 connections per domain.) Click on Advanced Delivery tab and enter your domain to masquerade it. Specify a Smart host and configure external DNS servers (limit to three) to perform reverse lookup.

Current Sessions and Queues objects of SMTP enable administrators to manually terminate all active sessions and connections in Exchange server. Local delivery queue, directory lookup queue, and messages-to-be routed queue provide valuable information that is essential when troubleshooting an SMTP problem or sleuthing a security compromise. Right-click on local queue to freeze/unfreeze messages, delete messages (with or without NDR notice), and to define and set a custom filter.

## First Storage Group

Mailbox Store

Enable "Zero out deleted database pages" to purge pages from disk by going to Properties of first storage group. Avoid using circular logging as it will reuse log files instead of archiving using separate 5-MB log files. Mailbox Store supports archive of messages for mailboxes, which I recommend that you do and store critical event- or log-based message offline for future evidence against a hacker. (If you haven't set up a dedicated logging database server and mailbox to receive event notifications, then I suggest that you add this project to your to-do list.) Make sure that "Client support for S/MIME signatures is enabled. Confirm that "This database can be overwritten by a restore" check box is cleared on the Database tab, and customize maintenance interval to run daily from 2 a.m. to 6 a.m. In the Limits tab, specify a mailbox size for users and protect your server (and users) from an attack that attempts to exponentially grow your store. Specify storage limits that meet your company's existing and long-term message requirements. Enable the check box "Do not permanently delete mailboxes and items until the store has been backed up". Check the Security tab to confirm that list of names is the previous list we customized when we removed the group Everyone.

Public Folder Store

Similar to Mailbox Store, confirm that the "Clients support S/MIME signatures" check box is checked, the maintenance interval is set to a custom schedule, storage limits are enforced, and items cannot be deleted until store has been backed up. In addition, avoid using the default of "Always run" for Replication interval. Depending on the size of your organization, you may want to set this interval to run frequently or to never run and manually force replication. In the Public Folder Instances, set the replica age limit (e.g., globalevents, internal, storeevents, etc.) to a minimum of 30 days or another limit more appropriate for your organization. Remove the group Everyone from Public Folders and manually add unique groups and users.

# First Routing Groups

SMTP Connector

Let's check the security of your SMTP connector included in your routing groups. Select the check box "Do not allow public folder referrals" to restrict referrals to other connector servers. In Content Restrictions tab, set limitation on message size allowed through. Avoid using "Always run" for the Connection time and select "Use different delivery times for oversize messages (if supported) to specify an alternative connection time. Make sure that the "Send HELO instead of EHLO" check box is cleared. Set Integrated Windows Authentication and TLS Encryption for outbound security. Check the "Do not send ETRN/TURN" to avoid processing messages for other clients. Set messages from everyone to be rejected by default and manually add each user that is allowed to send messages. I know that this is a tedious step but it will prevent a hacker from creating a new mailbox and sending messages in your organization.

# Be First Not Last

Be the first to know how your company mail server will respond by testing its security for holes on an ongoing basis. Make sure that you have covered the basic security steps, such as:

1. Using unique folder locations for your Exchange Server files.
2. Using the appropriate folder and file permissions.
3. Using restricted user/mailbox permissions and quotas.

4. Using a secured—instead of an out-of-the-box—mail server configuration.

As the mail administrator, it's important that you have the following:

1. An in-depth understanding of existing and potential security issues.
2. An ongoing dynamic security plan in place that addresses new threats.
3. An overall awareness of the security test results from consistent penetration testing against your mail server(s).

Make sure that you follow company protocol and adhere to policies and procedures before taking the initiative to address the need for penetration testing against your company's ongoing security. Consult with your IT manager first to develop a team-based security and test plan.

Is your Exchange 2000 Server running in Mixed Mode or Native Mode? Do you have a thorough understanding of your server configuration? Does this configuration precisely reflect your organizational structure? Unless your running a combination of Exchange 5.x and Exchange 2000 servers in your network, your server operation mode should be set to Native Mode, and not Mixed Mode.

In some cases, a software development company may need to maintain an Exchange 5.x server in their QA department to test their MAPI application for backward compatibility. Although your corporate mail server is secured, what about the mail server(s) in your QA subnet or other parts of the company?

You will need to take development, staging, and other QA servers that are accessible from the Internet into account when securing your corporate Exchange 2000 Server.

| Security Tips |
| :---: |
| • Consider security of other mail servers<br>• Remove routing groups<br>• Restrict delegation<br>• Apply 4-R Rule |

Not only should you eliminate unwanted routing groups/connectors (that is, other mail systems) to connect to your Exchange server, you should also keep the assignment of delegation control to the "chosen few", to avoid the "too-many-hands-in-the-cookie-jar" syndrome.

As you may already know, there is nothing preventing you (or another Exchange administrator) from assigning delegation control of the Exchange server to the group "Everyone" for the following roles: Exchange Administrator, Exchange Full Administrator (administer server plus permissions) and Exchange View Only Administrator. To assign administration delegation, launch Exchange System Manager, right-click on your Organization object and select Delegate Control.

## To MIME or not to MIME

An often-overlooked area is the MIME content type extensions registered in Exchange by default. It's critical that you understand that MIME content types utilize your Exchange Store and not just e-mail anymore. Program associations at this level can allow a browser (that is, Internet Explorer), an Outlook client, and an Outlook Express client to launch a program (e.g., Word) automatically. Unless your firewall administrator is blocking certain MIME content types at the firewall level, your Exchange server will allow your mail clients to automatically start up any program specified in Internet Message Formats.

To modify the list of MIME content type, start up Exchange System Manager and de-collapse Global Settings object. Then, right-click on Internet Message Formats and select Properties. Carefully review the list of extensions associated with content type and modify according to your environment.

No doubt users want to be able to send and receive files and not have to worry about size limitation imposed on their messages. However, just as it is vital to add a connection limitation on static rules defined in your firewall, setting limitations on your mail server in Message Delivery for Outgoing Message Size, Incoming Message Size, and Recipients Limits is also crucial.

| Security Tips |
| --- |
| • Avoid "unlimited" values<br>• Enforce limitations<br>• Check server logs<br>• Filter e-mail messages |

In my opinion, keeping the default value of "unlimited" or "no limit" for any parameter on any server is asking for trouble—at a minimum, a hacker can potentially use this against you.

To enforce limitations, right-click on Message Delivery and select Properties. Then, go to the Defaults tab and enter an appropriate value that reflects your environment for each field.

You'll want to check your mail server logs and with your firewall administrator to obtain historical reports (60-90 days back) about inbound/outbound sessions to your mail server(s). In addition, you can check with your company's ISP for additional traffic information to your site. All of these sources can provide you with the information that you'll need to find realistic values that are appropriate for your server configuration.

| Security Tips |
| --- |
| • Add e-mail filters<br>• Prevent delivery<br>• Return to sender<br>• Block e-mails |

By default, Exchange does not filter any e-mail. To prevent delivery of a message based on a sender, go to Filter tab in Message Delivery and enter the sender's e-mail address to block future e-mails from a specific sender.

## Recipient Policies

Use caution when making changes in Exchange since it can impact part or all of Active Directory objects. Consult with your IT Manager to define an effective recipient policy for your organization. Make sure that you follow company protocol and adhere to policies and procedures before taking the initiative to address the need for customized recipient policies.

When was the last time you checked your Exchange Recipient Policy and Filter Rules? Are you still using Microsoft's default recipient policy and filters on your Exchange server?

Create one or more recipient policies and define filters for existing and new users in your Exchange Organization. Instead of accepting Microsoft's default policy, modify or customize the policy to reflect your existing environment. In Exchange System Manager, go to

Recipients folder, de-collapse the folder and click on the Recipient Policies object.

If you're using Microsoft default policy, you'll see the "Default Policy" with Priority set to "low" and in the General tab a filter rule of (mail-nickname=*). Right-click on Recipient Policies object and select New to create a new policy. Once you have completed your policy, remember to right-click on the policy to "Apply this policy now" and make it active.

## E-mail Address Types

Prevent administrators from inadvertently generating incorrect addresses and users from accessing other unsecured mail systems. Remove unnecessary e-mail address types defined in the Generation Rules section of the E-Mail Addresses tab.

## Global Address Security

Beneath the Recipient Policies icon, you'll find "All Address Lists" and "All Global Address Lists" on your left pane. You'll need to right-click each one, select Properties, and then go to the Security tab to view a list of groups and users with permissions. (Remember to test changes in a staging network and not in a live network.) Ensure that the groups Everyone and Authenticated Users do not have Full (or other special) permissions.

## Inheritable Permissions

Replace the group "Everyone" with "Authenticated Users" and if possible, remove the Everyone object from inheriting any permissions. To accomplish this, click on the Everyone object and deselect "Allow inheritable permissions from parent to propagate to this object". You will be prompted to Copy or Remove or Cancel. Select Remove to replace inheritable permissions with explicitly specified permissions for the Everyone object. You'll need to remove this object from the "All Address Lists" and "All Global Address Lists".

## Update Service

This service is responsible for processing updates to your address lists and maintains recipient modifications made in your Exchange environment. You will notice two services: Recipient Update Service (Enterprise Configuration) and Recipient Update Service (your domain name). Make sure that you customize the update interval to reflect your organization's update requirements, instead of accepting the "Always run" default value. Why create additional network traffic if it is not necessary?

| Security Tips |
| --- |
| • Avoid "always running" |
| • Closely manage interval |
| • Set up custom schedule |
| • Manual force updates |

Avoid "always running" the Recipient Update Service at the cost of mail server security. Closely manage the update interval by choosing when updates will occur in your organization.

Customize when Active Directory services will propagate updates in your network. You may find that running recipient list updates overnight is not required, and that propagating changes at that time can assist a hacker.

Set up a custom schedule to update changes during your company's hours of operations (for example, between 8 a.m.–6 p.m.) You should also create a schedule for the Offline Address List. Remember you can always right-click on the service and select "Update Now" to force an update throughout your domain. My preference is to manually force updates; however, this may not be practical solution depending on your organizational structure.

Note: To rebuild and "recalculate the Address List membership and the Recipient Policy settings of all recipients in your domain in the next scheduled update interval", select "Rebuild".

| Security Tips |
| --- |
| • Begin at the firewall |
| • Find traffic volume |
| • Set maximum limitations |
| • Monitor traffic volume |
| • Stay current with hotfixes |
| • OWA encryption |

How do you begin to protect your mail server at the firewall? By identifying the maximum simultaneous connections recorded or logged to your mail servers(s) and enforcing that in your firewall static route/object entries for each mail server.

Mail server security requires an understanding of the latest traffic volume to each mail server?

Why allow unlimited connections in the firewall to your SMTP server, if your syslog server has never logged more than 100 simultaneous connections to the mail server? Why allow more connections in the firewall to your Outlook Web Access (OWA) server than configured OWA users? These are just two servers (out of many) that can benefit from an embryonic limit; that is, a maximum connection limitation imposed in your firewall static entries for your mail server and OWA server objects.

Your firewall policy should reflect the minimum connection requirements (with some room for growth) of your servers, where the value of
maximum connections is NOT set to unlimited. Companies using
Outlook Web Access (OWA) enable their Exchange server to be accessible via a front-end web server and an Internet browser on the client
side. Don't even think about running OWA without using Secure
Sockets Layer (SSL) or port 443 and requiring128-bit encryption.

Stay current with service packs and security hotfixes to ensure that
security exploits or known bugs in your mail server are patched. Failure
to keep current can result in a security compromise of your mail server
and/or electronic messages (e-mail). Are you logging your e-mail subjects and tracking messages?

Your Exchange 2000 Server provides an option to log e-mail subjects,
track messages, and store tracking information to a log file (stored in
your Exchsrvr\<servername>.log folder). These additional options are
not enabled by default. Consider enabling both options to assist you
with better message tracking as part of your overall security plan.

As with other logging options, take into account any server performance overhead (e.g., disk, memory, and processor usage), and make sure
that your server has the capacity to handle the additional logging—in
particular, services and protocol logging, which we will cover later.

| Security Tips |
| --- |
| • Enable message tracking |
| • Restrict read access |
| • Unshare tracking folder |

One of the benefits of message
tracking is that you can track
(similar to doing a tracert on a
IP address) the path that an e-

mail takes to other e-mail systems and search by e-mail subjects, senders, and/or recipients.

Being able to collect this additional information now can assist you later—not only in tracing an e-mail security issue, but also assist you in troubleshooting a message delivery problem.

Make sure that you unshare this message-tracking folder and restrict read access to administrators only. In your <servername>.log folder in Exchsrvr, you will find the message tracking log file (e.g., 20021118) that you can open with Notepad to view the following fields:

Date, Time, client-ip, Client-hostname, Partner-Name, Server-hostname, server-IP, Recipient-Address, Event-ID, MSGID, Priority, Recipient-Report-Status, total-bytes, Number-Recipients, Origination-Time, Encryption, service-Version, Linked-MSGID, Message-Subject, Sender-Address.

Use Message Tracking Center and define the messages that you want to track in logs moving forward. Increase your log file maintenance to remove log files after 14 days and archive off-site for long-term retrieval. (Microsoft recommends removal of log files after 7 days; however, I have found that doubling their recommendations works better for me most of the time.) To enable subject logging and message tracking, right-click on your Exchange server listed under the Servers container of the First Administrative Group in System Manager. In the General table, click on each option and then set "remove files older than" to 14 days, instead of 7 days. You may find that setting the maximum age longer than 14 days is more practical in your Exchange organization. Remember to hit the Apply button in order for your new changes to take effect. Once you have enabled Message Tracking Center (MST), go to Tools and right-click on MST to create a message tracking.

Add your Exchange server and then define your criteria for tracking message(s). You may need to modify the following Registry key to update the working (e.g., tracking.log) folder:

HKEY_LOCAL_MACHINE\SYSTEM\CurrentControlSet\Services \MSExchangeSA\Parameters\LogDirectory

The last option on the General tab is the "This is a front-end server", which allows you to enable your Exchange server as a relay—that is, an Outlook Web Access—server. This mode supports client connectivity via the Internet Explorer browser; however, it exposes your Exchange server to a whole new level of security threats.

| Security Tips |
| --- |
| • Avoid relay server<br>• Use VPN to get e-mail<br>• Use OWA if you must |

Don't even think about converting your existing Exchange server to a front-end relay server. Instead, set up your Exchange server to be accessible to your remote users through a Virtual Private Network (VPN) connection.

A less desirable option (in my opinion) is to set up a secured and dedicated front-end IIS web server and enforce 128-bit encryption using the Secure Socket Layer (SSL) over port 443. Port 80 connections should never be accepted to your Exchange OWA server.

Make sure that you update your firewall policy to only permit port 443 through to your front-end IIS web/OWA server. Block all the other TCP/IP ports and set a maximum connection limitation in your static route (or address translation entry) to your mail server. Avoid using unlimited values for your maximum connections.

A less desirable option is to set up the front-end IIS web server outside your firewall and configure your perimeter router to only permit port 443 through. In either case, your firewall policy will need to be updated and traffic filtering will need to be done in your perimeter router.

Periodically check the text box "Domain controller used by services on this server" on the General tab to make sure that the name of the DC that manages user access is your AD root (first installed) server. You will want to control which server manages user access in your domain; if this server changes, you want to be the first to know.

Although Microsoft has made some improvements by enabling more security features in their applications out-of-the-box, no services logging are enabled in Exchange 2000 Enterprise Server, by default. At a minimum, you will need to define the diagnostic logging, message tracking, and monitoring of events, messages, and services required in your organization.

## Outlook 2000 Clients

Let's take a moment to review the configuration of your Outlook 2000 clients. I'll begin by setting up a new Outlook client using the startup wizard. Click on the Microsoft Outlook icon that is created after an Office or Outlook installation. Select the "Corporate or Workgroup" option, the Exchange Server, and then to "Manually configure information services".

Change the default Profile Name of "MS Exchange Settings". Add the Exchange Server and appropriate Address Books as services for the new profile you created. Avoid adding other services (such as Internet

E-mail, Fax Mail Transport, etc.) to corporate e-mail profiles. Use a dedicated profile for the other services. Once you have specified the Exchange server, mailbox, and performed Check Name, select to "Manually control connection state" and the "Choose the connection type when starting".

Microsoft defaults to automatically detect connection state upon startup, which I don't suggest you do. In manual mode, Outlook will require human intervention to proceed, making it difficult for a hacker's program or process to launch your Outlook automatically. Keep in mind that Outlook will prompt your users to connect or work offline every time they start up their e-mail.

In the Advanced tab, you will notice that you can add additional mailboxes to open under one profile. Make sure that you regularly monitor user mailboxes and identify who has access to open other mailboxes. (I once detected that a certain VP was inadvertently opening up one of my engineer's mailbox without knowing it. This kind of mailbox access must be granted through a formal process.)

| Security Tips |
| --- |
| • Encrypt communications<br>• Select NT authentication<br>• Permissions and roles |

An often-overlooked setting is the "Encrypt information" for Outlook clients using the network and/or dial-up networking. Make sure that you enable this for all of your users and select NT Password Authentication for logon network security.

Change the default offline folder path, file name, and select the Best Encryption option (with your disk compression) to protect your users offline folder. Remember to add the services Global Address Book,

Personal Address Book, and Personal Folders (with password) to your newly created profile. Know the Permissions and Roles of your Inbox Properties. In Outlook, go to File, then Folder, and select Properties for "Inbox", then go to the Permissions tab.

How secure is your e-mail communications?

## S/MIME

At a minimum, install/import a digital certificate and use Secure MIME (S/MIME) to secure your e-mail communications (content and attachments). Go to Security tab In Options, under Tools and click on Setup Secure E-mail. Type a name for your settings name, select S/MIME for message format, then click on the New button to create your settings. Enable default security setting for message format and for all secure messages. Next, you'll need to choose the digital certificate you installed previously for signing and for encrypting. (Check out Verisign's Go Secure for Microsoft Exchange for more information. Depending on your organization, you may opt to use Exchange Server Security for message format instead of S/MIME.)

## Security Zone

Select the appropriate security zone for your organization, which will control the behavior of security zone-aware programs (such as Outlook and IE), and reduce the potential harm of unsafe content delivered to your users. Microsoft's default security level for the Internet zone is Medium; however, I suggest that you experiment with the security level High—which provides the most security—for each zone.

Keep in mind that this security level will affect some of the web sites that you visit. An often-overlooked area is the Trusted Sites zone. You may want to consider reviewing and adding your company's business partner secured (https) websites to your security zone and set to security level High. Consider adding non-secured sites that your company does not want users visiting in the Restricted Sites, again with the security level set to High.

## Medina's 4-R Rule of Administration

When in doubt as to deciding if a network administrator should be assigned privileges to administer part or your entire server, consider using my 4-R rule of administration as a guide. The 4-R rule of administration is, retire or renew based on role or requirements. Now is the time to verify who's on your delegation list and to renew/retire accounts based on the current role/requirements.

## What If It's True?

Ever wonder if hackers pitched their "tent of meeting" near your IT camp? Like Moses and the Israelites, are you wandering in the wilderness in search of security and the promised LAN—a network safe and secure from the bondage of hackers? Have you implemented layered security, or is there a divine pillar of cloud guiding your company with network security?

The historicity of Moses' life (and death) can be observed for physical evidence, that explains the natural and spiritual phenomena; he experienced thoughts, feelings, and a will to serve the Creator of creation and witness miracles. Is not the life (or death) of man physical evidence that he existed?

If anyone accepts materialist philosophy—and rejects biblical truths—as part of their indoctrination, then the philosophy or theory of physical matter (thought, feeling, mind, will, etc.), as the only reality, exists only in the present state, and not in the past.

Moses provided evidence that physical phenomena or supernatural forces do not constitute the highest value in life, that only through a relationship with the Creator—who holds that nothing exists without His creation—is the spiritual phenomena conceivable, beyond the framework of nature. Moses proved this prior and subsequent to his death, when he appeared with Elijah after Jesus' transfiguration.

Is Microsoft your Internet Messiah?

# Chapter 7

## Desktop Security

| O/S Security |
| --- |
| • /etc/services <br> • Port 139 & 445 <br> • Your data <br> • Cipher command <br> • Windows 2000 Pro <br> • Windows 2000 services <br> • Windows XP services <br> • IE 6 browser security <br> • Automatic Updates <br> • Outlook connection |

One of the most overlooked areas of network security is the local and remote desktop. An often-overlooked area at this level (host) is the Operating System (O/S) security, TCP/IP or network related configuration and files (such as the lack of IP filtering and the use of the default /etc/services file), and software application security.

Recent attacks have circumvented firewall security via Internet browsers, e-mail applications, and file attachments.

The new security frontier is an undeveloped field exposed to the dark forces of hackers. Attacks are designed to take advantage of misconfigured hosts running with outdated patches and missing critical security hotfixes. Users are no longer protected from hackers by a network firewall or conventional security alone. The viable venue for a hacker's paradise is any application resident in memory on a host (desktop or laptop) outside or behind a firewall. Malicious code (executable code) coupled with Trojan horses (destructive programs) operate under the guise of normalcy to recruit hosts and gain an involuntarily start from users. New attacks are difficult to detect as hackers utilize new methodologies to confound the wise all the while delivering a large-scale attack on the Internet. Regardless of a hacker's objective—whether to facilitate an attack from your computer to another site, or to obtain confidential information from your company, hackers are determined to go the distance and traverse your network seeking security vulnerabilities.

To combat the existing desktop attacks, consider installing a desktop firewall on remote (VPN and dial-up) hosts. However, a desktop firewall is another application and, if improperly configured or not properly maintained, can become the weakest security link in your network. A desktop firewall should address the above attacks and other desktop-specific attacks. When tackling network security, it's imperative that you implement a layered security approach that protects hosts from threats against any of the 7 layers (Physical, Data Link, Network, Transport, Session, Presentation, and Application) of the OSI model, which servers use to communicate over TCP/IP networks and the Internet. The type of security associated with each layer is defined better by asking what potential attacks exist at each layer; below is a list of some of the attacks:

| | |
|---|---|
| Application attacks | Distributed DoS (DDoS) and spoofing |
| Presentation attacks | DDoS and spoofing |
| Session attacks | DDoS and spoofing |
| Transport attacks | DoS and hijacking |
| Network attacks | Spoofing of IP & poisoning of ARP |
| Data Link attacks | Overload of MAC table and port |
| Physical attacks | Sniffing and severing of backbone |

# /etc/services

Why maintain a file with known services and default ports that you don't want your users to connect to? Consider reviewing your services file and making the appropriate modifications to reflect your security environment. I have included below a sample services file for your corporate and remote users. If a new service is not included in the services file, add it and then change the default port to restrict usage of it. The /system32/drivers/etc/services file located in the system root folder of your Windows 2000/NT server or in c:\windows folder in other versions of Windows, controls what services and ports your users can access (locally or remotely). Customize the services file and change the default ports for well-known services, for example, if you don't want a user to connect using the native FTP client program, change the default port of 21 (control) and 20 (data) to unique numbers (e.g., 6521 and 7520). This change would require that the destination FTP server is listening on the same unique ports in order for your users to connect and use this service. The services file defines for your users, which port(s) each service will open to communicate with another server or service. If there is a service defined in this file, the computer will most likely accept an inbound connection from a remote host to the defined service, unless TCP/IP filtering is configured and blocking the IP address of the remote host. Services like FTP (port 21) and Telnet (port 23) will allow your users to connect with another server on your LAN or on the Internet (if your firewall and border router permit these services through).

# Port 139 & 445

Control what services your users can access by changing the default port number in the /services file. Begin restricting usage of ports here and also in your firewall and border routers. Keep in mind that

NetBIOS over TCP/IP (port 139) is not secured and should be blocked from inbound or outbound access through the firewall to the Internet/DMZ for security reasons. To allow this port through the firewall is to defeat the purpose of having a firewall in the first place. Windows NT uses Port 139 for null sessions and for file sharing; Windows 2000 uses (for SMB) port 445 if port 139 is not enabled.

## Sample Services file

| Service | Port | Alias | Comment |
|---|---|---|---|
| *Add a service here* | *Change port* | *Don't use alias* | *Don't use comments* |
| ftp-data | 7520/tcp | | #FTP, data |
| ftp | 6521/tcp | | #FTP. control |
| telnet | 5523/tcp | | |
| smtp | 25/tcp | mail | #SMTP |
| tftp | 6569/udp | | #Trivial File Transfer |
| http | 80/tcp | www www-http | #World Wide Web |
| pop3 | 110/tcp | | #Post Office Protocol-Ver 3 |
| https | 443/tcp | MCom | |
| https | 443/udp | MCom | |
| syslog | 6514/udp | | |

**Security Tips**

- Add a new service
- Change service port
- Move services file
- Set file to Read-only
- Enable auditing

Add a new service to this file and/or change the default port to control usage of service. Next, set file permission to read-only and if necessary move file to another folder location. Then, enable auditing to monitor successful or failure attempts to modify this file.

## Your data

If your data is worth backing up then it is also worth securing. Regardless of your user's operating system or client configuration, your entire network security depends on how well you secure the local and remote entry points to the infrastructure, such as desktop and laptop users with access to network shares. Consider the following when thinking about network security for your company:

- First, educate your users on computer and data security in a timely manner and provide a medium for users to contact you in case of a security violation.
- Second, keep your users well informed of potential security exploits and remind them of the dos and don'ts of computer and data security while at work and at home.
- Third, define a security process for handling user-level and company-wide level security issues and establish a forum for disseminating security information.
- Fourth, publish an internal security newsletter and solicit user input and feedback and address any concerns at the user-level and company-wide level.

See chapter one (combating attacks) for client attack types to watch out for.

## Cipher Command

Use command-line program Cipher to encrypt your folders and files. Type "cipher" alone without qualifiers to display a list of folders and files encrypted (E) or unencrypted (U). Type "cipher /?" to get a list of parameters and command syntax to use; for example, /e = encrypt, /d = decrypt, /s=includes subdirectories, and /k = create new file encryption key: Type cipher /e /s: "<directory or file name>.

| Security Tips |
| --- |
| • Use Cipher to encrypt<br>• Avoid using drag-and-drop for files |

For example, "cipher /e /s: temp" sets the directory temp to encrypt new files created in this directory; however, files copied to the temp (or other encrypted) folders using drag-and-drop will not be encrypted, by default. Run the cipher command again.

## SAM & Syskey

Encrypt your SAM file with SYSKEY and select the option to store the encrypted key on a floppy disk. Keep in mind that the floppy disk will be required during the system boot phase. Storing the encrypted key on the local drive is not as secure, since there are utilities available to manipulate the password hash. Make a backup of the floppy disk and store in a safe, in case your original floppy disk gets damaged.

Your company should have a user security policy in place that describes the services offered by various operating systems and explains the implications of running each service. It's important that your users understand what services are required and should only be running on their home computers while connected to your network. After all, their home computer is another entry point into your infrastructure. Make sure that they disable unnecessary services for security reasons and to free up system resources.

## Windows 2000 Professional

Remote users running Windows 2000 Professional operating system and connecting to your network via VPN should keep their computers up to date with service packs, security hotfixes, and anti-virus protection. I've included below some of the services that I would disable by default:

## Windows 2000 Services

| | |
|---|---|
| Alerter | Network News Transport Protocol |
| Application Management | Plug and Play |
| Automatic Updates | Print Spooler |
| Background Intelligence | Print Spooler |
| Clipbook | Remote Procedure Call (RPC) |
| Computer Browser | Remote Procedure Locator |
| DHCP Client | Remote Registry |
| Distributed File System | Removal Storage |
| Distributed Link Tracking System | Server |
| Distributed Link Tracking Server | SMTP |
| Distributed Transaction Coordinator | Task Scheduler |
| DNS Client | TCP/IP NetBIOS Helper |
| Fax Service | Telephony |
| File Replication Service | Telnet |
| IIS Admin Service | Terminal Services |
| Indexing Service | Windows Management |

Internet Connection Sharing
Intersite Messaging
Logical Disk Manager
Messenger
Microsoft Search
Net Logon
NetMeeting Desktop Sharing
Network Connections

Windows Management Driver
Windows Media Monitor Service
Windows Media Program Service
Windows Media Station Service
Windows Media Unicast Service
Windows Time
Workstation
WWW Publishing Service

## Windows XP services

Remote users running XP operating system and connecting to your network via VPN should keep their computers up to date with service packs, security hotfixes, and anti-virus protection. I've included below some of the services that I would disable by default:

NOTE: Make sure users have a full backup of their system before making changes.

- Application Layer Gateway Service—if not using Internet Sharing
- Automatic Updates—this can work for you or against you; at some point, someone will hack this process to propagate an attack on your system
- Background Intelligent Transfer Service—used by Windows Update
- Error Reporting Service—self explanatory
- Internet Connection Firewall—unless you are sharing Internet
- NetMeeting Remote Desktop Sharing—enable when you need it
- Remote Access Auto Connection Manager—unless sharing Internet
- Remote Desktop Help Session Manager—enable when you need it

- Remote Access Connection Manager—unless sharing Internet
- Routing and Remote Access—unless sharing Internet
- TCP NetBIOS Helper Service—used for WINS
- Terminal Services—enable when you need it
- Upload Manager
- WebClient

| Browser Security |
| --- |
| • Microsoft On-Demand |
| • Privacy On-Demand |

Is your Internet browser spun on the woven path of a hacker's warped web? Are your users exploring the web or trapped in a hacker's sequence of motifs?

Will your company's dominant theme in 2003 be browser security or compromised privacy? Like in the book of Job, is your trust [security] fragile and are you leaning on a spider's web? (Job 8:14-16)

## Microsoft On-Demand

By default, Microsoft enables "Install On Demand" to allow your Internet Explorer browser version 6.0 to download and install plug-ins/components automatically using IE Active Setup. Although your browser will prompt you before proceeding with download/install of object(s), it is possible for hackers to use IE setup against you and launch an attack or carry out a particular task in your browser. Not to mention, you have not verified the integrity of the installable component and are relying on Microsoft (or other vendors in the case of IE version 5.x).

Instead of relying on your browser to prompt your users for downloads, installs, and/or updates, consider disabling these features and implementing a company policy that only propagates these components once your security administrator has completed the following three steps:

1. Manually downloaded each component from the vendor's official web site.
2. Verified the official release of component and original file size with vendor.
3. Tested off-line and certified component is safe to distribute to your users.

Start securing your user's browser today by clicking on the Restore Defaults button located in the Tools\Internet Options\Advanced tab to reset advanced settings. Then, go to the Browsing section and clear the following features:

- Enable Install On Demand (Internet Explorer)
- Enable Install On Demand (Other)
- Automatically check for Internet Explorer updates
- Reuse Windows for launching shortcuts
- Closed unused folders in History and Favorites
- Enable folder view for FTP sites
- Enable offline items to be synchronized on a schedule
- Enable third-party browser extension
- Show friendly HTTP error messages
- Use passive FTP (for firewall or DSL modem capability)

When was the last time you re-checked your browser security settings?

In the General tab, click on the Settings button and then Move Folder button to specify a unique path to store your Temporary Internet Files folder. Next, change "Check for newer versions of stored pages" from

Automatically to "Every visit to the page". Consider resetting the amount of disk space to use to 1MB only.

You will be prompted to log off in order for Windows to finish moving files to new location. Make sure that you save your work environment and then select Yes; otherwise, your settings will revert back to default values. Log in and verify (in Settings) the path for Temporary Internet Files folder is the one you specified. Click on View Objects folder and remove any unused objects. Take note of the date and file size for each object and check periodically for any discrepancies.

In the General tab, click on Delete Cookies then Delete Files (select offline content) to clear all of the cookies and temporary files stored in your Temporary Internet Files folder. Next, clear the History folder and set "Days to keep pages in history" to zero.
Make sure that you take the time to set the appropriate permissions and enable auditing on Temporary Internet Files folder. At a minimum, enable successful and failed auditing of the following activities:

- List Folder / Read Data
- Read Attributes & Read Extended
- Create Files / Write Data
- Create Folders / Append Data
- Write Attributes / Write Extended
- Delete Subfolders / Delete
- Change Permissions

## Privacy On-Demand

Consider changing the default setting of Medium for Privacy to High and then managing the websites that your browser will accept or block cookies from. Set the privacy level to Block All Cookies and decide if you want to override cookie handling to restrict websites from inserting or reading a cookie on your computer in the first place.

## Automatic Updates

Avoid running the Windows Update Service to automatically update your server since this process can be hacked. If you decide to use this service, then set it to notify you before downloading and installing any update! Visit Security & Privacy section at www.microsoft.com/security and download the following tools to assist you with security updates:

- Baseline Security Analyzer: Scans your server for common security misconfiguration.
- HFNetChk: Command line tool that identifies the current patch level of your server and missing patches.
- IIS Lockdown: Disables unnecessary IIS features.
- URLScan: Works in conjunction with IIS Lockdown to restrict HTTP requests.

In addition to maintaining your operating system updated with the latest service pack and security hotfix, native and third-part applications and drivers need to be patched to address security holes.

## Outlook Connection State

Set Outlook to "Manually control Connection State" and the "Choose the connection type when starting". Microsoft defaults to automatically detect Connection State upon startup, which I don't suggest that you do. In manual mode, Outlook will require human intervention to proceed, making it difficult for a hacker's program or process to launch your Outlook automatically. Keep in mind that Outlook will prompt your users to connect or work offline every time they start up their e-mail client. See chapter six (Exchange 2000 Server Security) for more information on securing Outlook 2000 Clients.

# Chapter 8

# Profile of Hackers & Stalkers

| Sleuthing the hackers |
| :--- |
| • What do hackers want? |
| • Solomon's response |
| • The New Messenger |
| • Age-old battle |
| • 4-P cycle of hacking |
| • Individualistic culture |
| • Sophisticated hackers? |
| • Sleuthing the stalkers |

Is your production or corporate network an open invitation to hackers everywhere? How do you know that a hacker hasn't responded to the challenge and taken control of your company's entire network(s)?

In this chapter, we will focus on the profile of sophisticated hackers and Internet Stalkers.

As Mr. O'Reilly at the Factor on Fox would say, "Caution: You're about to enter a no spin zone." What you're about to read may cause you to think more seriously about sophisticated hackers (and their quest to control your systems/data), and about Internet Stalkers (and their quest to invade your privacy).

## What Do Hackers Want?

Ever wonder what hackers are up to next? One response is, "I'm too busy doing my job and applying security hotfixes…" yet hackers want dominion over your network—and ultimately, ascertain your company's data—not your job! Security hotfixes can be a red herring if you're trying to determine what new technology a hacker will utilize next.

## Solomon's Response

While you're busy applying hotfixes for recently exploited programs, hackers are "manufacturing" the next "Killer App" or hacking tool, to decide the fate of your job or your company's presence on the Internet. Solomon wrote in the book of Ecclesiastes 1:9:

*"What has been will be again, what has been done will be done again; there is nothing new under the sun."*

## The New Messenger

The Internet is the new messenger of our civilization; it is the electronic carrier of our communications and global marketplace for the 21st century. The concept of a messenger and human communications is nothing new though; both have been around since the beginning of civilization.

## Age-old Battle

For good or evil, the Internet has the infrastructure to deliver both causes—yet this age-old battle is nothing new, but an ongoing struggle for many who have succumbed to the temptations of unethical practices on the Internet and in business.

You don't have to look very far today to see the financial burden hackers impose on some businesses, and the corporate "book cooking" going on by some CFO's, to understand that the consequences of management corruption have lasting repercussions in the organization's culture, its employees, and inevitably the company's reputation.

How does this relate to network security? A Company in turmoil makes for an easy target, and employees with technical expertise—threatened by unemployment—may seek revenge through hacking methods and/or disseminating confidential information in a public forum.

## 4-P Cycle of Hacking

| Medina's 4-P Cycle of Continuous Hacking |
| :--- |
| The 4-P cycle is Patience, Possession, Power, and Pleasure: <br><br> • Patience—hackers take anywhere from minutes to months to achieve their goals <br> • Possession—the hacker's reward; the targeted company's stressor <br> • Power—control of systems and data <br> • Pleasure—the reinforcement of continuous hacking |

For young novice and experienced hackers, the obsession begins as a challenge and is reinforced by the adrenaline rush (what I call the 4-P cycle of continuous hacking) experienced during each intrusion.

Sophisticated hackers appear to be invincible and flawless in their attacks, and unlike some addicts in need of a quick fix, hackers are patient and determined to stake out your network, one host at a time.

Tracking down and prosecuting hackers will not solve all of our security problems:

For example, applying Deming's 85-15 rule will show that about 85% of security failures are due to system breakdowns in layered security management beyond the network administrator's immediate control while administrators are responsible for security failures 15% of the time.

## Individualistic Culture

Unlike monochronic cultures and polychronic cultures, hackers are of the individualistic culture and think primarily in terms of "I" and "me". Initial port scans begin the process of collecting network information that is then organized to identify potential security holes.

Hackers are methodical in approaching their targets and in planning their network attacks. They understand that knowledge of the following areas of their target is essential to build a basic framework to workaround:

1. Business culture
2. Network configurations
3. Partner connections
4. Hours of operations

## Sophisticated Hackers

> **Medina's Profile of Sophisticated Hackers:**
>
> - Understands the business culture of their targets
> - Recognizes the potential security holes
> - Exercises patience and collects pertinent information
> - Plans and organizes the attacks
> - Manages the hacking process and controls details
> - Applies new techniques to combat security measures
> - Evaluates attack outcome and their performance
> - Enhances technical skills and defines new objectives

### Hacking Trends

Hacking technologies incorporate one or more of the following characteristics:

- Propagation through automations
- Faster discovery/roaming programs
- Firewall and wireless pseudo (friendly) packets
- Distributed server and client agents

### Hacking Targets

- Anti-virus & patch/hotfix programs
- IE, Outlook, and OWA
- IIS and SSL
- Cisco routers and firewalls
- VPN clients
- Wireless

### Hacker Types

- Script kiddies
- Intermediate
- Experienced/Sophisticated

| Sleuthing the stalkers |
| :--- |
| • Quest for Newbie |
| • Quest for Pedophile |
| • Quest for Predator |
| • What if it's true? |

Another culture exists on the Internet today, but unlike hackers, these predators—also known as Internet Stalkers—want more than access to your computer, they are on a mission to invade your privacy and to threaten your world.

While you are busy keeping hackers out of your network, an Internet Stalker may be creeping into your life.

How do you know that a stalker hasn't already obtained access to your private information? Is there a Goliath invading your privacy or threatening your world today? Is someone stalking the security administrator? Similar to hackers, there are at least three different kinds of stalkers roaming the Internet seeking whom to devour.

## Quest for Newbie

Similar to script kiddies (novice hackers), these Internet stalkers have limited technical capabilities and operate in a random fashion scouring the Internet for vulnerable users registered in chat rooms and in public forums. The script kiddies-stalkers probe (often copying other probing tactics) for personal information and quickly move on if resistance is detected along their search path.

Although these stalkers appear to be harmless, nevertheless, they are on a quest to learn more information about you than you are prepared to divulge to strangers.

## Quest for Pedophile

Similar to experienced hackers, who are electronically attracted to your data, pedophiles are physically attracted to your kids. Unlike stalkers on a quest to learn, these stalkers are serious with the power to attract and lure other kids online. They hang out in chat rooms and in forums and appear on your screen disguised as another innocent kid online that just happen to find your kid. Eventually, the conversations turn into a subtle interrogation session with an invitation to an in-person meeting.

| Security Tips |
| --- |
| • Avoid using real name |
| • Use new nicknames |
| • Use new secret code |
| • Avoid sharing password |
| • Monitor your kids online |

Avoid using your family's real or known name online, especially in chat rooms, forums, or online gaming sites. Use new nicknames that only your close relatives know to identify and communicate with you. Use a secret code/theme to further verify that the other person is who he/she says they are.

Avoid sharing passwords and secret codes/themes and change this information frequently (e.g., every 15-30 days). Use a separate nickname for your friends and don't disclose your family's nickname to anyone outside your immediate family. Avoid meeting strangers online and monitor your kids' sessions in chat rooms, forums, and even with online gaming services as some now offer Chat services, such as Xbconnect.com.

Instruct your kids not to entertain any questions and instead direct all inquiries to you immediately. Observe your child's response behavior online periodically and verify—don't assume—that a relative, school-mate, and/or friend is indeed at the other end of the chat, forum, or game session.

## Quest for Predator

Similar to sophisticated hackers, predators thrive on invading your privacy and threatening your world. These stalkers are very serious about their mission and often like to show off how much knowledge they acquired about you. They observe your online and offline habits and become obsessed with you. In some cases, these stalkers will obtain enough information to break into your house.

Ask yourself the following questions:

1. Why is this type of stalker focused on you and/or your family?
2. How severe are the threats?
3. How much personal information has the stalker revealed to you?
4. Where online did you provide this private information?

| Security Tips |
| --- |
| • Meet with your family |
| • Contact local police |
| • Notify, notify, and notify |
| • Collect evidence |
| • Visit Cybercrime.gov |

First, meet with your immediate family to gather all the facts regarding any threats or computer crime(s) committed against you or one of your family members. Second, contact your local police department and make sure you report any threats, thefts, and behavioral patterns that you have observed from the stalker.

Notify your bank(s) and credit card companies as soon as possible and request new account numbers. Notify your manager at work and report any threats or computer crimes. Contact your University and report any threats or computer crimes. Contact and register a complaint with the ISP leasing the IP address to the stalker. Contact your ISP and consider changing ISP if they don't have an Internet abuse program in place or won't help you.

Collect emails from stalker and observe behavioral patterns (e.g., language patterns, word selections, and other characteristics) that could assist you in identifying the stalker at a later time. Change your host name, passwords, and contact your ISP to request that they renew your dynamic IP address with a different IP address and not just recycle your old IP address.

Visit "http://www.cybercrime.gov/reporting.htm" to learn if you are the victim of a computer crime and take the appropriate course of action. Consider using tools (e.g., automating "netstat–na >> log.txt" via scheduler) to monitor all of the connections to your computer. Confirm that your computer is running the latest software patches and security hotfixes. Closely monitors any chat rooms, forums, and gaming sites your kids participate in. Consider changing passwords/codes for home computers and alarm system.

No doubt, this is a psychological strain and a difficult process, however it is possible to track the Internet Stalker with good sleuthing and patience.

# What If It's True?

The threat from terrorists to our open society is prevalent today, but will the Internet be used as a vehicle to share and facilitate the information necessary to launch another attack? Who's patrolling the border to the information superhighway?

The events of 9/11 exposed the vulnerabilities in our airport security, the lack of information shared between the Central Intelligence Agency and the Federal Bureau of Investigation, and the threat to our open society. Vulnerabilities in our airport security have allowed terrorists to hijack our airplanes and convert them into missiles by crashing them into towers.

The vulnerabilities range from improper security checkpoint screening to an unprotected airplane cockpit. Airport security increase now requires that people arrive at least two hours early for the scheduled flight departure. People have to wait in line while thorough scans are performed. The world we live in is full of violence with pockets of terrorists in other countries. What if it's true that hackers and stalkers are carrying out some form of terrorism among children and Internet users across the world?

What if it's true that America is not prepared to protect itself from another massive terrorist attack on our soil or the Internet?

# Chapter 9

# — InfraSecurity Configuration Form

| Security Configuration Form |
| :---: |
| • Configuration template<br>• Recommendations |

Have you taken time to properly document and diagram your network infrastructure? When was the last time you updated your network documents and diagrams?

I have found that in almost every project I've consulted there has been poor or incomplete network documentation and outdated network diagrams. In this chapter, I will provide you with an infrastructure security configuration template to help you collect the correct information. However, collecting the configuration information is half the battle, you will need to maintain proper network documentation and diagrams.

# Infrastructure Security & Privacy Audit
Network Configuration Template
Version 1.0 (put date here)

Table of Contents

# 1. Perimeter Security

- Vendor/Model #:
- Router Name(s):
- O/S Version:
- ACL Security:
- Patch Level:
- Hotfix Level:
- Vulnerabilities Now:
- Available Version:
- Available Patch:
- Available Hotfix:
- External IP:
- Internal IP:

## Perimeter Security Recommendations:

Don't wait until your router is down to search for network topology documentation and outdated diagrams. Instead, be proactive and start (and maintain) a library of network information that can reduce your time in troubleshooting a network emergency.

# 2. Firewall Security

- Vendor/Model #:
- Firewall Name:
- O/S Version:
- Security Policy:
- Patch Level:
- Hotfix Level:
- Vulnerabilities Now:
- Available Version:
- Available Patch:
- Available Hotfix:
- External IP:
- Internal IP:

## Firewall Security Recommendations:

Avoid making new entries to your firewall policy if you can't review the recent changes done due to poor documentation. Separate new changes as much as possible to avoid confusion when an issue arises.

## 3. Intrusion Detection Security

- Vendor/Model #:
- IDS Name:
- O/S Version:
- Security Policy:
- Attack Signatures:
- Patch Level:
- Hotfix Level:
- Vulnerabilities Now:
- Available Version:
- Available Patch:
- Available Hotfix:
- Internal IP:

### Intrusion Detection Security Recommendations:

Are you recording new hack attempts to your servers and network? Begin recording suspicious probes and print a hardcopy of the top ten.

# 4. Cluster Security

- Vendor/Model #:
- Cluster Name:
- O/S Version:
- Security Level:
- Patch Level:
- Hotfix Level:
- Vulnerabilities Now:
- Available Version:
- Available Patch:
- Available Hotfix:
- External IP:
- Internal IP:

## Cluster Security Recommendations:

Update your documentation to reflect the actual number of cluster pools set up for your servers. Have you put together a network diagram that shows the link between your cluster pools and servers?

## 5. Front-end Web Server Security

- Standard Config:
- Vendor/Model #:
- Web Server Name:
- O/S Version:
- Security Level:
- Patch Level:
- Hotfix Level:
- Vulnerabilities Now:
- Available Version:
- Available Patch:
- Available Hotfix:
- Internal IP:

## Front-end Security Recommendations:

Can you quickly spot a server that lacks a recent service pack or security hotfix? You can, if your server documentation is kept up to date! Monitor your documentation.

# 6. Application Firewall Security

- Vendor/Model #:
- Application Name:
- O/S Version:
- Security Level:
- Patch Level:
- Hotfix Level:
- Vulnerabilities:
- Available Version:
- Available Patch:
- Available Hotfix:

## Application Firewall Security Recommendations:

Is there a critical IIS web server on your network without an application firewall running? Try to document your network changes at the time you make the changes.

## 7. Service/Process Security

- Vendor/Model #:
- Router Name:
- O/S Version:
- Security Level:
- Patch Level:
- Hotfix Level:
- Vulnerabilities Now:
- Available Version:
- Available Patch:
- Available Hotfix:

### Service/Process Security Recommendations:

Do you know the total number of services or processes that your application is running? Document the original timestamp of your service and process.

# 8. Back-end Security

- Vendor/Model #:
- Database Name:
- O/S Version:
- Security Level:
- Patch Level:
- Hotfix Level:
- Vulnerabilities Now:
- Available Version:
- Available Patch:
- Available Hotfix:
- External IP:
- Internet IP:

## Back-end Security Recommendations:

Monitor the normal and abnormal growth of your databases. Have you documented the normal trends of database usage within your organization?

## 9. Data Security

- Data size:
- Patch Level:
- Hotfix Level:
- Vulnerabilities Now:
- Available Version:
- Available Patch:
- Available Hotfix:

## Data Security Recommendations:

Keep track of internal changes made to massage your company's data.

## 10. VPN & WAN Security

- Provider:
- T1 Circuit ID:
- O/S Version:
- Security Level:
- Patch Level:
- Hotfix Level:
- Vulnerabilities Now:
- Available Version:
- Available Patch:
- Available Hotfix:
- Internet IP:

## VPN & WAN Security Recommendations:

Create a confidential network diagram that shows the VPN and WAN links to your network infrastructure. Include circuit ID number and other pertinent information to assist you when contacting service provider.

## 11. Remote Access Security

- Vendor/Model #:
- O/S Version:
- Security Level:
- Patch Level:
- Hotfix Level:
- Vulnerabilities Now:
- Available Version:
- Available Patch:
- Available Hotfix:
- Internal IP:

## Remote Access Security Recommendations:

Document all of your entry points to your network infrastructure and outbound links to other networks for remote administration.

## 12. Network Access Security

- AD/Domain Name:
- Security Policies:
- Procedures:
- Metabase:
- Registry:
- Vulnerabilities Now:
- Available Version:
- Available Patch:
- Available Hotfix:

**Network Access Security Recommendations:**

Where are your Active Directory objects? Keep track of your Active Directory changes by documenting your configuration.

## 13. Internet & DNS Security

- SOA / Provider:
- Domain Name:
- DNS Server Name:

- O/S Version:
- Security Level:
- Patch Level:
- Hotfix Level:
- Vulnerabilities Now:
- Available Version:
- Available Patch:
- Available Hotfix:
- Primary DNS IP:
- Secondary DNS IP:

### Internet & DNS Security Recommendations:

Avoid registering your primary, secondary, and cache DNS servers with the same ISP. For failover purposes, set up a cache server with another provider.

## 14. E-mail Security

- Vendor/Model #:
- Domain Name:
- O/S Version:
- Security Level:
- Patch Level:
- Hotfix Level:
- Vulnerabilities Now:
- Available Version:
- Available Patch:
- Available Hotfix:
- Internal IP:

### E-mail Security Recommendations:

Avoid unnecessary downtime due to a conflicting change to your mail server. Document your updates.

# 15. File Server Security

- Server Name:
- O/S Version:
- Security Level:
- Patch Level:
- Hotfix Level:
- Vulnerabilities Now:
- Available Version:
- Available Patch:
- Available Hotfix:
- Internal IP:

## File Server Security Recommendations:

Audit every file on your file servers and archive unused files offline.

## 16. Backup Security

- Offsite Provider:
- Server Name:
- Application Name:
- O/S Version:
- Security Level:
- Patch Level:
- Hotfix Level:
- Vulnerabilities Now:
- Available Version:
- Available Patch:
- Available Hotfix:
- Internal IP:

### Backup Security Recommendations:

Document your backup schema and avoid waiting to the last minute to test your backup tapes. Restore your backups frequently to avoid any surprises when you least expect it.

# 17. Anti-Virus Security

- Vendor/Model #:
- Schedule:
- Signature File:
- Patch Level:
- Hotfix Level:
- Vulnerabilities Now:
- Available Version:
- Available Patch:
- Available Hotfix:
- Internal IP:

## Anti-Virus Security Recommendations:

Help your users quickly by knowing the latest anti-virus signature files your hosts are using. Your documentation should include a list of users with outdated anti-virus engines or signature files.

## 18. Host Security

- Vendor/Model:
- Host Name:
- O/S Version:
- Security Level:
- Patch Level:
- Hotfix Level:
- Vulnerabilities Now:
- Available Version:
- Available Patch:
- Available Hotfix:
- Internal IP:

### Host Security Recommendations:

Avoid user downtime by staying current with security exploits. Document the patch and hotfix level of each host. Note any issues as a result of a new patch install.

# 19. Dial-up Security

- Vendor/Model #:
- Server Name:
- O/S Version:
- Security Level:
- Patch Level:
- Hotfix Level:
- Vulnerabilities Now:
- Available Version:
- Available Patch:
- Available Hotfix:
- Internal IP:

## Dial-up Security Recommendations:

Your network is mission critical, especially when a dial-up user introduces a new virus and it adversely affects your business. Communicate the dos and don'ts of network security with your users regularly.

## 20. Physical Security

- Personal Access: 
- Practices: 
- Passwords: 

### Physical Security Recommendations:

Is your network lab door open and are developers in and out of your lab? Avoid unnecessary traffic near your servers, especially production servers.

## 21. ISP Uplink Security

- Vendor/Model: 
- Connection Type: 
- Security Level: 
- Vulnerabilities Now: 
- Internal IP: 

### ISP Uplink Security Recommendations:

What's your ISP up to? Find out. Document any network latency and traffic patterns that affect your business.

## 22. Co-location Security

- Connection Type:
- Security Level:
- Vulnerabilities Now:
- IP addresses

### Co-location Security Recommendations:

Document your network routes between your headquarters and your co-location sites. Closely monitor your network path along your ISP's backbone.

## 23. Security Threat Management

- Standards:
- Policies:
- Procedures:
- Administration:
- Incident Response:
- Vulnerability Tests:
- Monitoring:
- Maintenance:

### Security Threat Management Recommendations:

Note any reference to other areas of documentation such as Standards, Policies, and Procedures. Include in your configuration template for future reference.

## 24. Disaster Recovery (DR) Plan

- Policy Guide:
- Primary Site:
- Standby Site:
- Connection type:
- Internal IP:

### Disaster Recovery (DR) Plan Recommendations:

Include a reference in your configuration template to point you in the proper location for specifics regarding DR plan.

## 25. Network Diagram

- Live Infrastructure:
- Future Upgrades:
- Redundancy Links:

### Network Diagram Recommendations:

Show your network connections and data flow in your network diagrams. Avoid using too much information that will clutter your presentation and make it difficult to depict critical links. Keep your network diagrams updated on a timely manner. Use a "before-and after" approach when working with network diagrams. Don't overwrite your old copy, do a "save-as" for store your changes in a new diagram.

# Security Q&A

**Security Q&A**

- Proxy links
- Firewall detecting hacks
- Website with PDFs
- XP retaining old IP
- Explain to Networking guys
- Get firewall back
- Secure SAM file

As the author of the Weakest Link Security series, I've had the privilege of responding to user questions from around the world.

## Question #1: Learn about proxy server

Hi! I have a question; Could you tell me about a page or link where I can start if I want to learn about proxy server, particularly with one running over Red Hat Linux. Thanks for your help!

Omalex78

## Answer:

Dear Omalex78:

Thank you for taking the time to pose your question. It's been my experience that some administrators have attempted to substitute a proxy server for a firewall (regardless of the operating system). In some cases, a proxy server had been installed because the firewall in place did not offer caching capabilities. In either case, I ask you to consider implementing a firewall or upgrading it to support caching. If you choose to implement a proxy server, beware of httptunnel.

Below are the proxy server links for Red Hat Linux:

Red Hat Stronghold version 3.x
http://www.redhat.com/docs/manuals/stronghold/Stronghold-3.0-Manual/admin-guide/chapter4.fm.html

Squid Web Proxy Cache 2.5
http://www.squid-cache.org

## Question #2: Firewall detecting hackers

Here is my question (or rather questions):
My firewall is detecting hacker attacks called netBIOS Browsing, ping attack and cloaking all the time. What does this mean? Is it dangerous? How do I stop this? Can I somehow put the hackers who are doing this behind bars?

Psycho

## Answer:

Dear Psycho:

Thank you for taking the time to pose your questions. NetBIOS (port 139) and Server Message Block (port 445—used if port 139 is disabled) are used for file sharing and provide information about your servers and sessions. These ports (along with ICMP/Ping) should be blocked in your border router, firewall, and disabled on servers with valid IP addresses that are accessible from the Internet.

Add a new rule in your router and firewall to drop any packets from the offending IP addresses (or network) scanning your network. Next, do a trace route (tracert) on these IP addresses and notify the ISP where the attacks are originating from—chances are the ISP may have been hacked and they don't know it.

As for the severity of the attempts, carefully consider the following:

1. Review your firewall logs as far back as you can and observe "accepted" connections and follow through.
2. Review your server logs for security compromise and enable auditing, if not already done.
3. Make a backup of your firewall logs and keep a printed copy available for quick reference.
4. Check your firewall settings and make sure it's properly configured (e.g., to prevent anti-spoofing).
5. Update your firewall and servers with the latest "tested" service packs and security hotfixes.
6. Visit http://www.cybercrime.gov/reporting.htm to learn if you are the victim of a computer crime and take the appropriate course of action.

7. Define alarms and configure your router, firewall, and servers to notify you immediately
8. Closely monitor your router, firewall, and server logs moving forward.
9. Read up on script kiddies.

## Question #3: Website with PDFs

Hello, I would be very grateful if you could help me on this one.
I have created a website that has some PDFs that can only be seen by subscribers; there are 3 kind of subscribers (for the moment). Depending on their subscription, they can see or not the PDF. This is managed by the login control. However, the problem is that whenever you login, you can see the address for the PDF; you can pass on this address to a friend and if he clicks on the link then he can see the pdf.

One solution is to put, on the private folder "allpdfs", an ASPX page that will check if the user is identified or not; if not identified then he will be redirected to a page to login, but if he is identified, then I make a copy of the requested pdf file into a public folder and redirect user to that copy to see it.

I don't like this solution, so if I want to show the identified user the original pdf file, then I have to set the access for the private fodler "allpdfs" to anonymous which is bad (all users can then see it)!

My question is: how can I manage to show the original pdf file within "allpdfs" folder by not having to play with the Anonymous access property of that folder (virtual root)? May be there is a way that security is only handled by my ASPX page…? I mean I wonder how the other websites do it?

Drelias

## Answer:

Dear Drelias:

Try turning off ASP caching (Go to IIS\Home Directory\ Configuration\App Options), restart your web server, and test login control again. Re-enable ASP caching and decrease your session time-outs.

If subscription access to PDFs requires subscribers to manually authenticate then consider creating a separate folder for each subscriber, use NT authentication (not clear text), and assign a unique password for each dedicated folder. That way, even if a friend obtains the address, they will be required to authenticate in order to view PDF files. You will not need to move PDF files from a private folder to a public folder, since you have set up a dedicated folder (with unique password) for each subscriber.

## Question #4: XP retaining old IP address

Under WINXP Home edition I am at a loss—My Web Host changed IP location, but when I run a ping or tracert, it still comes up as the old IP #. I know it is not my ISP, as I have a win2000 and a WINME system using a router switch to my cable. I have flusheddns and cleared all caches I know of. What in XP would retaining old IP addresses?

Any help is greatly appreciated!

Metcalf

## Answer:

Dear Metcalf:

Thank you for taking the time to pose your question.

If you are using DHCP on XP, have you released and renewed your old IP address?

If you ran a ping and tracert on the local XP computer and it returned the old IP#, then check the hosts and lmhosts files located in the folder c:\windows or c:\winnt\system32\drivers\etc\. (Run a search on these files to make sure you've located all the copies.) Next, check TCP/IP settings to see what DNS and/or WINS servers are specified. If XP is configured for DHCP, you will find that your router or another server is providing most (if not all) of the TCP/IP configuration. I don't think the router is the problem. Check to make sure your XP computer is not inadvertently pointing to another computer for DNS or WINS. If you ran a ping and tracert on your Windows 2000 or ME computer and it returned the old IP#, then check the above areas on your Windows 2000 and ME.

Is your XP computer configured with a valid IP address? In other words, do you have a valid registered host name for the XP that is accessible from the Internet?

# Question #5: XP Explain to networking guys

As DBA, I need to be able to go to my Networking guys and tell them what I am doing and why. Why do you not want IIS on the same box? Why do you not want client for MS installed, etc. I am trying to get up to speed on server security and any way you can point me in the right direction would be appreciated.

Ray

# Answer:

Dear Ray:

First, let me thank you for reading my security series, and for considering taking the necessary steps, to reduce the security risks with your database server—It appears you have identified your first security weak link, and are prepared to address this issue with your Networking department.

As for "how can I go about figuring out the why's?", you want to make sure that you first have a thorough understanding of the application and database requirements in your organization. In other words, ask your key people the following questions with respect to IIS and client for MS: Is IIS required on your database server to handle a specific functionality? (I'd be concerned if you found that IIS is configured; if it is not configured, then someone may have inadvertently installed it and didn't understand the application requirements at the time.) Is client for MS required? This is installed by default and is used to allow your database server to browse your network; if it is not required, I would remove it.

The reason why you don't want IIS on the same box is for the obvious inherent security issues that exist with port 80; for example, why set up your database server to propagate the automation of a WORM on your network from other IIS servers inside your firewall? It's also possible that whoever set up IIS on your database server is also running FTP service, by default. I understand that your database server is behind a production or corporate firewall, but it doesn't justify running unnecessary services.

Once you have identified that IIS is not required, I would suggest that you plan and schedule a time after-hours to test your database server without WWW and IISADMIN services running, to see if your application will continue working. You may want to set the above services to manual and reboot your database server, before you determine the services are not necessary. As for MSDTC and other services, I suggest you carefully do your homework and stage stopping the services (one at a time), until you've achieved running only the required services on your database server.

It looks like you are thinking about taking the initiative, to secure that database server. I would schedule a meeting with the key people in your organization, to explore (and stage) the existing configuration of your server. Remember to make (and test) a full backup of your server before making modifications.

You'd be surprised by what you and others will learn when you go beyond the surface level of your server configuration.

## Question #6: Get firewall back

I have a small network (20 workstations) with the server running NTServer4 and the WS's have Win98SE. I use System Policy Editor to control the users to some extent, but I'm afraid I don't have a firewall. I had WinProxy on a proxy server, but it stopped working correctly and I got rid of it. Now the network is hooked up direct by way of a LinkSys box and a WaveLAN Manager box. How can I get a firewall back? BTW, I also use an HP managed switch. The router plugs into that. <8-O

E-bert

## Answer:

Dear E-bert:

Sorry to hear that your proxy server is not working. Hopefully you recorded any error messages and exhausted all of your troubleshooting options to salvage it. The critical issue now is having your network connected to the Internet without a real firewall. My first suggestion would be to invest in a hardware firewall solution (e.g. PIX) and implement an effective security policy. Keep in mind, the expense to recover from a potential network attack (even for 20 desktops) can be twice the cost of your initial firewall investment. A security violation is a matter of when (and not if) it will happen in the near future. In the interim, enable filtering on your LinkSys Router and block ports that you are not using. Check with LinkSys, Agere Systems, and Microsoft for any new patches or hotfixes and apply as needed.

## Question #7: Secure SAM file

DEAR SIR
How can I secure my SAM file on XP? I am sharing my pc in pear to pear environment.

Manoor

## Answer:

Dear MANOOR:

You can encrypt your SAM file with SYSKEY and selecting the option to store the encrypted key on a floppy disk. Keep in mind that the floppy disk will be required during the system boot phase. Storing the encrypted key on the local drive is not as secure, since there are utilities available to manipulate the password hash. Make a backup of the floppy disk and store in a safe, in case your original floppy disk gets damaged.

# Sample Configurations

| Sample Configurations |
|---|
| • Production Cisco router |
| • Production Cisco PIX Firewall |
| • /etc/services file |
| • OSI Model |

This section includes the production router and firewall security configurations used in this book. These configurations have been tested and used in critical networks. Each sample shows you how to make your router and firewall more secure.

If your Cisco router or firewall lacks the rules in the sample configuration listed below, then you have found your first security weak link. Remember to make a backup of your existing *running-config* before making any changes to your routers and firewalls.

Let's examine the router sample configuration file. Only anti-spoofing, anti-DoS, and NBAR lines will be covered, therefore this is a partial file; it assumes that you understand how to install an ACL.

## Production Cisco Router Configuration

> ! Sample config file with access-list 112 for inbound packet filtering.
> ! Enable only the services that are absolutely required; disable all others.
> ! Although some services are enabled by default, understand the role of each service.
> **service password-encryption** ! Uses basic algorithm to encrypt enable password
> ! Avoid using these services (DEC): Discard, Echo, and Chargen.
> **no service tcp-small-servers**
> **no service udp-small servers**
> ! Disable finger and Cisco discovery protocol (router sends info about itself)
> **no service finger**
> **no cdp running**
> **no cdp enable**
> ! Make sure you disable http and SNMP access for remote configuration and monitoring.
> ! Encrypt your password, disable http to your router, and define your syslog server.
> **enable secret 5 <password>** ! Uses MD5 password hashing for admin access.
> **no ip http server** ! Unless you want to send cleartext password, or the equivalent.
> **logging <syslog server>** ! If you haven't set up a server, Kiwi Syslogd is pretty good.
> ! Don't even think about installing an access-list if this line is not one of your rules.
> ! This rule allows inbound access only when the connection is initiated from inside.

---

**access-list 112 permit tcp any <your network> <inverted mask> established log**
! This rule allows domain name resolution so users can browse the Internet.
! If possible, limit this rule to your ISP's DNS servers.
**access-list 112 permit udp any eq domain any log**
! Restrict pings from specific outside hosts to your servers.
! The implicit deny rule in effect when you use an access list will deny other icmp types.

**access-list 112 permit icmp host <outside host> host <your server> echo log**
! It's important to note that some services such as FTP use more than one TCP port.
! If you have to use FTP, change default ports of 21 and 20 (data) whenever possible.
**access-list 112 permit tcp any host <your server> eq 443 log**
! The firewall adds an implicit deny rule after your permit rules; no need to add this line.
! When limiting inbound access, make sure you open up the appropriate ports for VPN.
**access-list 112 deny ip any any**
**eq domain any log**

---

The purpose of my book is to explore the various areas in your network and bring to the surface any security vulnerabilities that have been overlooked. The intention of this chapter is not to tell you how to set up a router, but to point out the areas you should be aware of when configuring a Cisco router.

## Production Cisco PIX Firewall Configuration

If your PIX firewall policy accepts unlimited connections or has no embryonic limits defined for your servers, then you have found your first security weak link. Below is a sample configuration file to improve the security of your firewall. Remember to make a backup of your firewall and test your security rules.

```
! Sample PIX 5.34 Firewall config
! See static entries below for maximum and embryonic limits
nameif ethernet0 outside security0
nameif ethernet1 inside security100
enable password <PWD>encrypted
passwd <PWD> encrypted
hostname <HOSTNAME>
fixup protocol ftp 21
fixup protocol http 80
fixup protocol h323 1720
fixup protocol rsh 514
fixup protocol smtp 25
fixup protocol sqlnet 1521
fixup protocol sip 5060
no fixup protocol rtsp 554
names

! Access list for servers defined in static list below
access-list outside_in permit tcp any host <YOUR MAIL SERVER>
eq smtp
access-list outside_in permit tcp any host <YOUR OWA SERVER>
eq 443
access-list outside_in permit tcp any host <YOUR IIS SERVER> eq
80
```

```
no pager
logging on
logging timestamp
no logging standby
no logging console
no logging monitor
no logging buffered
logging trap informational
no logging history
logging facility 22
logging queue 512
logging host inside <SYSLOG>
interface ethernet0 100full
interface ethernet1 100full
mtu outside 1500
mtu inside 1500
ip address outside <INTERFACE> <MASK>
ip address inside <INTERFACE> <MASK>
ip verify reverse-path interface outside
ip audit info action alarm
ip audit attack action alarm
no failover
failover timeout 0:00:00
failover poll 15
failover ip address outside 0.0.0.0
failover ip address inside 0.0.0.0
arp timeout 14400
global (outside) 1 interface
nat (inside) 1 0.0.0.0 0.0.0.0 0 0
```

```
! Maximum connection is set to 100 and embryonic to 25 for SMTP
& OWA servers
static (inside,outside) <Valid IP> <YOUR MAIL SERVER> net-
mask 255.255.255.255 100 25
static (inside,outside) <Valid IP> <YOUR OWA SERVER> netmask
255.255.255.255 100 25
static (inside,outside) <Valid IP> <YOUR IIS SERVER> netmask
255.255.255.255 1000 100

access-group outside_in in interface outside
route outside 0.0.0.0 0.0.0.0 <default gateway> 1
timeout xlate 3:00:00
timeout conn 1:00:00 half-closed 0:10:00 udp 0:02:00 rpc 0:10:00
h323 0:05:00 si
p 0:30:00 sip_media 0:02:00
timeout uauth 0:05:00 absolute
aaa-server TACACS+ protocol tacacs+
aaa-server RADIUS protocol radius
no snmp-server location
no snmp-server contact
snmp-server community public
no snmp-server enable traps
floodguard enable
no sysopt route dnat
isakmp identity hostname
terminal width 80
```

The purpose of my book is to explore the various areas in your network and bring to the surface any security vulnerabilities that have been overlooked. The intention of this chapter is not to tell you how to set up a firewall, but to point out the areas you should be aware of when configuring a Cisco PIX firewall.

## Sample Services file

If your services file is using default ports, then your clients will be able to launch any native programs and attempt to use services such as FTP or Telnet to access other internal hosts or servers on the Internet. Control what services your users can access by changing the default port number. Begin restricting usage of ports here and also in your firewall and border routers.

| Service | Port | Alias | Comment |
|---|---|---|---|
| *Add a service here* | *Change port* | *Don't use alias* | *Don't use comments* |
| ftp-data | 7520/tcp | | #FTP, data |
| ftp | 6521/tcp | | #FTP. control |
| telnet | 5523/tcp | | |
| smtp | 25/tcp | mail | #SMTP |
| tftp | 6569/udp | | #Trivial File Transfer |
| http | 80/tcp | www www-http | #World Wide Web |
| pop3 | 110/tcp | | Post Office Protocol-Ver 3 |
| https | 443/tcp | MCom | |
| https | 443/udp | MCom | |
| syslog | 6514/udp | | |

## OSI Model

The Open Systems Interconnect (OSI) model consists of 7 layers (Physical, Data Link, Network, Transport, Session, Presentation, and Application). The type of security associated with each layer is defined better by asking what potential attacks exist at each layer; below is a list of some of the attacks:

| | |
|---|---|
| Application attacks | Distributed DoS (DDoS) and spoofing |
| Presentation attacks | DDoS and spoofing |
| Session attacks | DDoS and spoofing |
| Transport attacks | DoS and hijacking |
| Network attacks | Spoofing of IP & poisoning of ARP |
| Data Link attacks | Overload of MAC table and port |
| Physical attacks | Sniffing and severing of backbone |

# About the Author

Luis F. Medina has over 15 years of network support experience and 10 network certifications (MCSE, Master CNE, CCNA, Unix CNE and more) and has worked as a network consultant, IT Manager, network engineer and administrator supporting and securing Cisco, Windows 2000, NT, Unix, NetWare, TCP/IP and the Internet.

0-595-26494-8

www.ingramcontent.com/pod-product-compliance
Lightning Source LLC
Chambersburg PA
CBHW051237050326
40689CB00007B/962